The

Bhagavad Gita

The
Bhagavad Gita

The Original Sanskrit

and

An English Translation
Lars Martin Fosse

YogaVidya.com

YogaVidya.com, PO Box 569, Woodstock NY 12498-0569 USA

First edition

The Latin dedication means "For Sarolta Eva Maria, my dearest daughter."

⊗ The paper used in this book meets the requirements of the American
National Standards Institute/National Information Standards Organization
Permanence of Paper for Publications and Documents in Libraries and Archives,
ANSI/NISO Z39.48-1992.

Manufactured in the United States of America

British Library Cataloguing-in-Publication Data
A catalogue record for this book is available from the British Library.

Library of Congress Cataloging-in-Publication Data
Bhagavadgita. English & Sanskrit.
  The Bhagavad Gita : the original Sanskrit and an English translation /
Lars Martin Fosse. — 1st ed.
    p. cm.
Includes index.
ISBN 978-0-9716466-6-7 (cloth : alk. paper)
ISBN 978-0-9716466-7-4 (pbk. : alk. paper)
I. Fosse, Lars Martin. II. Title.
BL1138.62.E5 2007
294.5'92404521—dc22   2006052812

Loretta is the essential element.

Saroltae Evae Mariae carissimae filiae

Contents

Introduction

You are about to have the profound pleasure of reading one of the truly great books in the history of the world. Not only is it a spiritual monument—an essential scripture of Hinduism, recited daily for two millennia and to this very day, whose teachings have spread throughout Asia and around the globe—it is also a literary masterpiece, the linchpin of a great epic of war and peace, honor and disgrace, loyalty and betrayal. It is a book people everywhere in the world return to again and again throughout their lives for insight into the nature of reality.

For the Hindu philosophers, the Bhagavad Gita was always of great importance. It is one of the three central texts of Vedanta, the other two being the Brahma Sutras and the Upanishads. From the ninth century CE onwards, philosophers such as Shankara, Ramanuja, Madhva, and Nimbarka in the Vedanta tradition, and Abhinavagupta in the Shaiva tradition, wrote learned commentaries on the Gita. It was also translated from Sanskrit into other Indian languages, for example, Jnaneshvara's Marathi version in the thirteenth century. As a work of literature, the epic was immensely important to the cultural life of India and even beyond her shores, notably in Indonesia, where parts were translated into Old Javanese.

It was during the British Raj that the Gita first achieved worldwide fame. Many educated Indians were struggling to defend Hinduism against the onslaught of western culture, and gradually the Gita was considered to embody the essential spirit and deepest truths of Hinduism. The Hindu reformer Ram Mohun Roy referred to the Gita as "the essence of all shastras," or the essence of all scriptures. By 1912, C. F. Andrews could claim that the Gita had become a common and well-read scripture for the whole of educated India. It also appealed to another, and very different group of people, the Theosophists. It was the Theosophists who introduced the Gita to that most famous of all modern Indians: Mohandas K. Gandhi.

Since Gandhi was introduced to the Gita by the Theosophists, he learned to read it in an allegorical way. The mighty battle was really a struggle for truth—which he saw as another word for God—to be sought through love, and love ruled out violence. Ahimsa, or nonviolence, became the key to Gandhi's understanding of the Gita, which he called his "spiritual dictionary." He was particularly fascinated by two words: aparigraha (nonpossession), which suggested the renunciation of money and property to avoid cramping the life of the spirit; and samabhava (equability), which asked him to transcend pain or pleasure, victory or defeat, and to work without hope of success or fear of failure. The Gita became an inspiration to Gandhi and millions of his followers, a manual of devotion and action in the modern world.

The Gita also found a rapt audience in the West, and a fascinating global cross-fertilization followed. It appealed both to the German Romantics, notably Schlegel, Humboldt, and Goethe, and to the American Transcendentalists, a group in New England who thought that insights which transcended logic and experience would reveal the deepest truths. The Gita was first translated into English in India in 1785 by Charles Wilkins, a merchant with the East India Company, and his translation made a deep impression on the Transcendentalist's leader, Ralph Waldo Emerson. Emerson's poem, "Brahma," elegantly captures some of the essence of the Gita:

If the red slayer think he slays,
    Or if the slain think he is slain,
They know not well the subtle ways
    I keep, and pass, and turn again.

Far or forgot to me is near;
    Shadow and sunlight are the same;
The vanished gods to me appear;
    and one to me are shame and fame.

They reckon ill who leave me out;
    When me they fly, I am the wings;
I am the doubter and the doubt,
    And I the hymn the Brahmin sings.

The strong gods pine for my abode,
    And pine in vain the sacred Seven;
But thou, meek lover of the good!
    Find me, and turn thy back on heaven.

The poem is based on a verse found in both the Gita and the Katha Upanishad. (A century later, another great poet, T. S. Eliot, also had a lifelong interest in Indian philosophy and incorporated it into his poetry as well.) Emerson made the Gita required reading for all those who were in rebellion against evangelical Christianity. Thus, for the first time, the Gita became part of a counterculture.

Another Transcendentalist, Henry David Thoreau, was a tremendous enthusiast of the Gita, but his interest was also a practical one. He incorporated a version of the Gita's teaching on Karma Yoga into his own lifestyle and philosophy. In 1849, he launched the idea of civil disobedience—an idea that influenced Gandhi's political thinking. Thus, an Indic idea passed through a Western mind and returned transformed to India. (Similarly, the Theosophical Society was founded in New York City, moved its headquarters to India, and was a catalyst in the revival of Hinduism and Buddhism.) And of course, Gandhi's ideas flowed back westward to inspire two other giants of the twentieth century, Martin Luther King Jr. and Nelson Mandela.

The current tidal wave of interest in the Gita, in Yoga, and in things Indian began in the 1960s with the efflorescence of another counterculture, the paperback revolution in book publishing, the new, far-reaching curricula of a higher educational system undergoing explosive growth, and the arrival in the West of gurus such as Swami Vishnudevananda, Swami Satchidananda, and A. C. Bhaktivedanta, all following in the footsteps of Swami Vivekananda.

Today, the Bhagavad Gita is firmly established around the world as a true classic. But not a dusty old classic: It is astonishingly fresh and inspiring, even to readers who do not share the underlying assumptions of the text. Knowledge and self-discipline are still virtues. Selflessness is as sound today as it was then. Doing one's duty regardless of consequences is needed now more than ever. We may not share the Gita's views on caste or endorse the social system it supports, but we don't have to. We are free to choose, and the Gita offers a number of choices. Its core of universal values and its poetic grandeur make the Gita a living classic.

I mentioned earlier that the Gita is the linchpin of a great epic, and that epic is the *Mahabharata*, or Great Story of the Bharatas. With nearly one hundred thousand verses divided into eighteen books, it is one of the longest epic poems in the world—fully seven times longer than the *Iliad* and the *Odyssey* combined, or three times longer than the Bible. It is in fact a whole library of stories that exerted a tremendous influence on the people and literature of India.

The central story of the *Mahabharata* is a conflict over succession to the throne of Hastinapura, a kingdom just north of modern Delhi that was the ancestral realm of a tribe most commonly known as the Bharatas. (India was at that time divided amongst many small, and often warring, kingdoms.) The struggle is between two groups of cousins, the Pandavas, or sons of Pandu, and the Kauravas, or descendants of Kuru. Because of his blindness, Dhritarashtra, the elder brother of Pandu, is passed over as king, the throne going instead to Pandu. However, Pandu renounces the throne, and Dhritarashtra assumes power after all. The sons of Pandu—Yudhishthira, Bhima, Arjuna, Nakula, and Sahadeva—grow up together with their cousins, the Kauravas. Due to enmity and jealousy, the Pandavas are forced to leave the kingdom when their father dies. During their exile, they jointly marry Draupadi and befriend their cousin Krishna, who from then on accompanies them. They return and share sovereignty with the Kauravas, but have to withdraw to the forest for thirteen years when Yudhishthira loses all his possessions in a game of dice with Duryodhana, the eldest of the Kauravas. When they return from the forest to demand their share of the kingdom back, Duryodhana refuses. This means war. Krishna acts as counselor to the Pandavas. The Gita is found right here, with the two armies facing each other and ready for battle. The battle rages for eighteen days and ends with the defeat of the Kauravas. All the Kauravas die; only the five Pandava brothers and Krishna survive. The six set out for heaven together, but all die on the way, except Yudhishthira, who reaches the gates of heaven accompanied only by a small dog, who turns out to be an incarnation of the god Dharma. After tests of faithfulness and constancy, Yudhishthira is reunited in heaven with his brothers and Draupadi in eternal bliss.

It is within this enormous epic—the sizable book you hold in your hands is well less than one percent of the *Mahabharata* that we find the Bhagavad Gita, or the Song of the Lord, most commonly referred to simply as the Gita. It is found in the sixth book of the epic, just before the great battle between the Pandavas and the Kauravas. The greatest hero of the Pandavas, Arjuna, has pulled up his chariot in the middle of the battlefield between the two opposing armies. He is accompanied by Krishna, who acts as his charioteer. In a fit of despondency, Arjuna throws down his bow and refuses to fight, deploring the immorality of the coming war. It is a moment of supreme drama: time stands still, the armies are frozen in place, and God speaks.

The situation is extremely grave. A great kingdom is about to self-destruct in internecine warfare, making a mockery of dharma, the eternal moral laws and customs that govern the universe. Arjuna's objections are well founded: He is the victim of a moral paradox. On the one hand, he is facing persons who, according to dharma, deserve his respect and veneration. On the other hand, his duty as a warrior demands that he kill them.

Yet no fruits of victory would seem to justify such a heinous crime. It is, seemingly, a dilemma without solution. It is this state of moral confusion that the Gita sets out to mend.

When Arjuna refuses to fight, Krishna has no patience with him. Only when he realizes the extent of Arjuna's despondency does Krishna change his attitude and start teaching the mysteries of dharmic action in this world. He introduces Arjuna to the structure of the universe, the concepts of prakriti, primordial nature, and the three gunas, the properties that are active in prakriti. Then he takes Arjuna on a tour of philosophical ideas and ways of salvation. He discusses the nature of theory and action, the importance of ritual, the ultimate principle, Brahman, all the while gradually disclosing his own nature as the highest god. This part of the Gita culminates in an overwhelming vision: Krishna allows Arjuna to see his supernal form, the Vishvarupa, which strikes terror into Arjuna's heart. The rest of the Gita deepens and supplements the ideas presented before the epiphany—the importance of self-control and faith, of equanimity and unselfishness, but above all, of bhakti, or devotion. Krishna explains to Arjuna how he can obtain immortality by transcending the properties which qualify not only primordial matter, but also human character and behavior. Krishna also emphasizes the importance of doing one's duty, declaring that it is better to do one's own duty without distinction than to do another's duty well. In the end, Arjuna is convinced. He picks up his bow and is ready to fight.

Knowing a couple of things will make your reading easier. The first is that the Gita is a conversation within a conversation. Dhritarashtra begins it by asking a question, and that is the last we hear out of him. He is answered by Sanjaya, who relates what is happening on the battlefield. (It is actually more dramatic and wondrous than the previous sentence indicates. Dhritarashtra is blind. Vyasa, his father, offers to restore his sight so he can follow the battle. Dhritarashtra declines this boon, feeling that seeing the carnage of his kinsmen would be more than he could bear. So instead, Vyasa bestows clairvoyance and clairaudience upon Sanjaya, Dhritarashtra's minister and charioteer. As they sit in their palace, Sanjaya relates what he sees and hears on the distant battlefield.) Sanjaya pops up now and again throughout the book as he relates to Dhritarashtra the conversation between Krishna and Arjuna. This second conversation is a bit one-sided, as Krishna does almost all of the talking. Thus, Sanjaya describes the situation, Arjuna asks the questions, and Krishna gives the answers.

The second thing to be aware of is the profusion of nicknames, also known as epithets. Almost all other translations either omit them or normalize them for simplicity's sake. Thus, Hrishikesha, Keshava, Govinda, and many other names will be left out or just translated as Krishna, and Son of Pritha, Son of Kunti, Mighty-armed Prince, Bharata, and many other epithets will be omitted or reduced to Arjuna. To maintain fidelity to the original, I am retaining all of them. They also make the text more flavorful and interesting, provide insight into Indian culture, and indeed into the story itself. For example, Krishna uses epithets of Arjuna that remind him of his royal lineage, his prowess in battle, and so on, to ease his dejection. They are also meaningful to our Indian readers. If you find them confusing, please turn to the back of the book, where you will find a comprehensive glossary explaining all the names and nicknames. Many of these names are still in use, so you may well find some of your friends and acquaintances listed there.

Unfortunately, one thing I cannot do to make your reading easier is completely explain everything in the Gita. That would be beyond the scope of an introduction, or even an entire book. For devotees and scholars alike, the Gita—and all the questions it raises—can absorb a lifetime of study. The YogaVidya.com web site lists dozens of books for further reading. I can, however, alert you to one fact about the Gita that will save you a lot of anguish and frustration: It contradicts itself. This was recognized early on and was cited by Shankara as the reason for writing his commentary.

Many explanations have been put forward to explain how theism, asceticism, dualism, pantheism, pragmatic material-ism, Yoga, Vedanta, and even Buddhism, all got woven into the text. One is that, at the time the Gita was written, the various systems of philosophy were not yet rigid and standardized, nor conceived of as being mutually exclusive. Another is that it is a work of mysticism and devotion, and is not intended to be logical or systematic. Another is that the text has the practical aim of salvation and is content to tolerantly lay out a variety of options. A variation on this view is that the options are graded according to simplicity or difficulty, with the way of knowledge being the most difficult and the way of devotion being the simplest and most efficient. Still another is to assign a hierarchy of truths to the statements in the Gita, so that some tell a simple truth and others reveal a higher truth. It should be noted that we still live with intellectual inconsistencies and levels of truth even in the modern world. For instance, we simultaneously believe in and utilize the classical mechanics of Newton and the relativity theory of Einstein. Both theories are true at the same time, but not on the same level. The inconsistencies of the Gita may have been as undisturbing to the ancients as the inconsistencies in our own theories of reality are to us.

Who would've written such a complicated book? Indian tradition holds that the entire *Mahabharata* was written by Vyasa, and many traditional pandits still hold this view. Modern scholarship has arrived at a more complex answer: There is no single author or single date of composition, and it began as oral poetry. A reciter would have had to know the story, but his reputation depended upon his skill in bringing the traditional material to life. Then as now, a first-class narrator was much in demand. We know from other oral-poetry traditions that the same bard would present the same story in different versions, longer or shorter as it suited the occasion. Thus, in its oral form, the epic had a reasonably fixed core, but its performance was highly flexible, with additions, embellishments, and digressions made on the spot to please the audience. In addition, oral poets had at their disposal a large number of formulaic expressions that could be easily fitted into the epic's sixteen-syllable meter in which the length of only a few syllables was fixed. The original nucleus of the epic may have been the creation of a single bard, or possibly a small group of bards, but it is now irrecoverable. It is likely to have been substantially shorter than the *Mahabharata's* shortest recorded version of twenty-four thousand verses, although we shouldn't underestimate the ability of oral cultures to produce very long texts.

An educated guess would suggest that the origin of the *Mahabharata* lies sometime during the eighth or ninth centuries BCE, although some scholars consider the roots of the epic to be much older. Among the specialists, there is now general agreement that the oldest portions of the epic that have been preserved are not likely to be older than 400 BCE. On the other end, it is difficult to fix an upper limit for the *Mahabharata's* composition. The didactic portions of the twelfth book in particular seem to have been added very late, perhaps in the fourth century CE.

Looking more specifically at the Gita, most scholars think the oldest parts may go back to the third century BCE, whereas the theistic portions may stem from the middle or end of the second century BCE. Chapters twelve through fifteen may date from the first century CE, whereas chapter seventeen is possibly even younger. The Gita was likely composed somewhere in north-central India, perhaps in modern Haryana or western Uttar Pradesh. These conclusions would probably hold good whether we believe that the Gita was a work originally separate from the *Mahabharata*, as some claim, or that it was originally part of the great epic. Even if the Gita was not originally a single unit or part of the epic, it has by now been handed down and read that way for many centuries.

We don't know when the *Mahabharata* was first written down. Possibly it was a gradual process, where parts of the epic were put into manuscripts, whereas other parts were still transmitted orally. Whenever the process started, there were only two possibilities: in the north, birch bark was used; and in the south, palm leaves. These are brittle materials, and frequent recopying was required if the text wasn't to be lost. The earliest surviving manuscript is from the ninth century CE. An owner of a manuscript could do with it as he pleased, and books consisting of leaves bound together with string allow other leaves to be easily inserted. The quality of the copying varied with the scribe— a bad scribe might make errors, and a better scribe might subsequently improve the text. All these processes created a lack of consistency, so we should not be surprised at the great variety amongst the different versions, or recensions, of the text.

The Gita first rolled off a printing press before there were complete editions of the *Mahabharata* itself. As noted earlier, it was translated into English for the first time in 1785 by Charles Wilkins. The first Sanskrit edition came out in 1806 under the supervision of Sir William Jones. In 1823, the German scholar August Wilhelm von Schlegel produced a first-class edition of the Gita and added a Latin translation. The first printed edition of the *Mahabharata* was the so-called Calcutta edition, completed in 1839, which was based on the Bengali recension of the text. The next attempt was the Bombay edition, largely based on the recension in Devanagari script and completed in 1863. The Kumbhakonam edition of 1910 incorporated the southern recension.

This situation was clearly less than satisfactory, so one of the greatest scholarly undertakings of the twentieth century was begun in 1919 at the Bhandarkar Oriental Research Institute in Poona (now spelled Pune). No less than ten distinguished editors, initially led by V. S. Sukthankar, and a host of assistants labored for forty-seven years to produce the definitive edition of the *Mahabharata*. The objective was to reconstruct the oldest possible form of the text on the basis of hundreds of manuscripts collected from all over the Indian subcontinent and Indonesia. The resulting set of nineteen volumes, containing thirteen thousand pages, was completed in 1966. I am very pleased that the Institute granted us permission to include their definitive Sanskrit edition of the Gita in this book, and we have taken great pains to present it to you in the beautiful Devanagari script—an extremely rare event outside of India. I would also like to thank Dr. John Smith, who has made an electronic text of the *Mahabharata* available on the Internet.

The situation regarding English translations today is also less than satisfactory—in fact, quite surprisingly so, given that the Gita has been translated into English literally hundreds of times over the last two centuries. The publisher of YogaVidya.com carefully examined more than a dozen of the most highly regarded translations with an eye toward reissuing the best one. Instead, he found them astonishingly deficient. Some stayed so close to the Indic syntax that they were unreadable in English. Others strayed so far from the original text that they were merely unreliable paraphrases. Still others suffered from ugly transliteration or amateur versification. Some others were distorted by the beliefs or egoism of the translator. And yet others were deformed by their publishers' marketing departments, always on the lookout for new hooks and angles.

So the publisher asked me to have a go at it, and I have tried my best to sidestep these shortcomings and avoid introducing new ones. I made great efforts to produce a translation that is both highly accurate and true to the original Sanskrit. I refrained from using verse, since that would militate against the objective of accuracy. As previously mentioned, unlike almost all other translations, all the names and epithets have been retained. If the phrasing in a particular sentence strikes you as strained or odd, more often than not it is from attempting to stay true to the original. I did not gloss over the inconsistencies and difficulties in the Gita, nor did I cover up uncomfortable topics such as sacrifices, caste, sexism, and the morality of war. (Although usually read as the story of a man seeking insight and salvation, the Gita can also be read as the story of a man with a conscience being taught to forget it.) And when questions arose, I consulted both Shankara's and Ramanuja's commentaries. At the same time, I sweated over every word, phrase, and punctuation mark to make the translation as clear and smooth as possible, using up-to-date terminology and international standard written English. Finally, I dispensed with footnotes so that you could relish this great work of literature without interruptions. Again, consult the bibliography online if you wish to delve deeper into the philosophical issues in the Gita.

Now for some specifics. The Indic conceptual system is very different from the Western system: It is often well-nigh impossible to find English terms that are semantically coextensive with the Indic terms. All translations of Sanskrit philosophical terms are therefore approximations, and many are disputed. Moreover, the exact meaning of a word is also determined by the philosophical and religious context in which it is used. Although other translators have made other choices in some instances, I have chosen to translate jnana with knowledge, vijnana with discrimination, and vidya with wisdom or science, depending upon context. I have chosen to translate the term guna with property, which I believe gives a better meaning than the often-used quality or constituent. Since sattva causes illumination because of its purity, I have chosen to translate the term with clarity rather than purity or goodness. Rajas, often translated as passion, I have translated as agitation in order to better bring out the physical aspect of the term. As for tamas, I have chosen sluggishness, again to emphasize the physical aspect. I have translated siddhas as perfected ones and karma mostly as action. However, karma has become an English loanword meaning "consequence of action." Where I found this to be the meaning, I have rendered karma as karma.

I have chosen to keep the Indic term Brahman even though it is not a normal loanword in English. The reason is that we don't have any word that really comes close to Brahman. The German scholar Paul Hacker sees it as primeval matter, but this in my opinion brings it too close to prakriti, which I have translated as primordial nature. Primeval energy may be better, but is not entirely satisfactory either: the immovable pole star, for instance, is identified with the unchanging Brahman. In the Vedas, Brahman relates especially to the power inherent in the mantras. A later text, the *Hiranyakeshi Grihyasutra*, says it is the navel of the universe and the navel of the pranas (breaths). Generally, Brahman stands for the Absolute, the source of everything, and is sometimes understood as a nonconscious principle, and sometimes as a conscious one, or God. The term, quite simply, can be interpreted many ways. I have therefore preferred to give this brief explanation of the term Brahman rather than translate it. Its adjectival form is Brahmic.

The word Yoga in various forms occurs almost one hundred and fifty times in the Gita. It is a complex term, and allows for a number of different interpretations, all dependent upon the context. The basic meaning is yoke—Yoga is in fact etymologically related to the English word yoke—but through various metaphorical processes the word came to cover a much wider semantic field. The Gita predates by a few centuries classical Yoga as we know it today, so in the Gita the word Yoga most often means simply mental discipline, or just discipline or training, while a yogi is a master of such discipline. It also refers to more specific forms of discipline, such as Karma Yoga (which I translated as the discipline of action) and Bhakti Yoga (translated as the discipline of devotion), and to creative or magical power. In the colophons, Yoga means a reflection or meditation upon a given subject.

In the end, a translation is always an interpretation, but an interpretation is not always a translation. The only way to get a truly intimate understanding of a Sanskrit text is to learn Sanskrit. Just by the way, although its concepts can be slippery and elusive, the vocabulary and grammar of the Gita are actually quite straightforward. If you were to learn Sanskrit, you could read the Gita in the original quite early in your studies. That is one very important reason why we included the Sanskrit in this book.

You may be interested to know that each chapter of the Gita was originally untitled. We have followed the traditional practice of pulling chapter titles from the colophons, those delightfully flowery sentences that bring each chapter to a satisfying close. Each and every chapter title could have begun with "The Yoga of" but we omitted this phrase to avoid excessive repetition and confusing constructions. We also took the opportunity to shorten and simplify the colophons, which can be very long and highly complex.

Finally, casting aside for a moment the historical conundrums, the scholarly debates, and the technical minutia, just know one thing: You are about to read one of the world's truly great books. It is essential reading for a nontrivial understanding of Hinduism, of India, and indeed of life itself. The Bhagavad Gita still speaks to people everywhere—across the oceans, across the millennia, and across the boundaries of language, religion, and culture.

Arjuna's Despair

धृतराष्ट्र उवाच ।
धर्मक्षेत्रे कुरुक्षेत्रे समवेता युयुत्सवः ।
मामकाः पाण्डवाश्चैव किमकुर्वत संजय ॥ 1

Dhritarashtra said, "When my troops and the sons of Pandu,
eager to fight, were arrayed on the Kuru field, the field of law,
what did they do, Sanjaya?"

संजय उवाच ।
दृष्ट्वा तु पाण्डवानीकं व्यूढं दुर्योधनस्तदा ।
आचार्यमुपसंगम्य राजा वचनमब्रवीत् ॥ 2

Sanjaya said, "When Duryodhana, the king, saw the army of
the Pandu sons assembled, he went to his teacher and spoke
these words.

पश्यैतां पाण्डुपुत्राणामाचार्य महतीं चमूम् ।
व्यूढां द्रुपदपुत्रेण तव शिष्येण धीमता ॥ 3

'Look at this huge army of the Pandu sons, teacher, arrayed for
battle by the son of Drupada, that brilliant student of yours.

अत्र शूरा महेष्वासा भीमार्जुनसमा युधि ।
युयुधानो विराटश्च द्रुपदश्च महारथः ॥ 4
धृष्टकेतुश्चेकितानः काशिराजश्च वीर्यवान् ।
पुरुजित्कुन्तिभोजश्च शैब्यश्च नरपुंगवः ॥ 5
युधामन्युश्च विक्रान्त उत्तमौजाश्च वीर्यवान् ।
सौभद्रो द्रौपदेयाश्च सर्व एव महारथाः ॥ 6

Here are the heroes, the great archers, the equals of Bhima
and Arjuna in battle: Yuyudhana, Virata, and the great warrior
Drupada; Dhrishtaketu, Chekitana, and the heroic king of
Kashi; Purujit, Kuntibhoja, and Shaibya, bull among men;
Yudhamanyu the bold and the heroic Uttamaujas; Saubhadra
and the sons of Drupada—all of them great warriors.

अस्माकं तु विशिष्टा ये तान्निबोध द्विजोत्तम ।
नायका मम सैन्यस्य संज्ञार्थं तान्ब्रवीमि ते ॥ 7

But, best of Brahmins, hear about our superior men, the
leaders of my army. I will mention them by name.

भवान्भीष्मश्च कर्णश्च कृपश्च समितिंजयः ।
अश्वत्थामा विकर्णश्च सौमदत्तिस्तथैव च ॥ 8
अन्ये च बहवः शूरा मदर्थे त्यक्तजीविताः ।
नानाशस्त्रप्रहरणाः सर्वे युद्धविशारदाः ॥ 9

You yourself, Bhishma, Karna, and Kripa, victor in battle;
Ashvatthaman, Vikarna, as well as the son of Somadatta, and
many other heroes willing to sacrifice their lives for my sake,
all battle-hardened wielders of many kinds of weapons.

अपर्याप्तं तदस्माकं बलं भीष्माभिरक्षितम् ।
पर्याप्तं त्विदमेतेषां बलं भीमाभिरक्षितम् ॥ 10

That force, protected by Bhima, is not a match for us, but this force, protected by Bhishma, is a match for them.

अयनेषु च सर्वेषु यथाभागमवस्थिताः ।
भीष्ममेवाभिरक्षन्तु भवन्तः सर्व एव हि ॥ 11

Indeed, it is Bhishma you must all protect along all avenues of approach as you man your respective positions.'

तस्य संजनयन्हर्षं कुरुवृद्धः पितामहः ।
सिंहनादं विनद्योच्चैः शङ्खं दध्मौ प्रतापवान् ॥ 12

In order to encourage him, grandfather, the majestic Kuru elder roared his lion's roar and blew his conch.

ततः शङ्खाश्च भेर्यश्च पणवानकगोमुखाः ।
सहसैवाभ्यहन्यन्त स शब्दस्तुमुलोऽभवत् ॥ 13

Then, all of a sudden, the conches, kettledrums, cymbals, big drums, and horns were sounded: It was a tumultuous noise.

ततः श्वेतैर्हयैर्युक्ते महति स्यन्दने स्थितौ ।
माधवः पाण्डवश्चैव दिव्यौ शङ्खौ प्रदध्मतुः ॥ 14

And standing on their great chariot yoked with white horses, Madhava and the son of Pandu blew their divine conches.

पाञ्चजन्यं हृषीकेशो देवदत्तं धनंजयः ।
पौण्ड्रं दध्मौ महाशङ्खं भीमकर्मा वृकोदरः ॥ 15

Hrishikesha blew his Pancajanya, Dhananjaya his Devadatta,
and Wolf Belly of terrible deeds blew the great conch Paundra.

अनन्तविजयं राजा कुन्तीपुत्रो युधिष्ठिरः ।
नकुलः सहदेवश्च सुघोषमणिपुष्पकौ ॥ 16

King Yudhishthira, the son of Kunti, blew his Anantavijaya;
Nakula and Sahadeva, their Sughosha and Manipushpaka.

काश्यश्च परमेष्वासः शिखण्डी च महारथः ।
धृष्टद्युम्नो विराटश्च सात्यकिश्चापराजितः ॥ 17
द्रुपदो द्रौपदेयाश्च सर्वशः पृथिवीपते ।
सौभद्रश्च महाबाहुः शङ्खान्दध्मुः पृथक्पृथक् ॥ 18

The Kashi king, the great archer, and the great warrior,
Shikhandi; Dhrishtadyumna and Virata and the undefeated
Satyaki; Drupada and the sons of Drupada: All together,
O Lord of the Earth, as well as the mighty-armed Saubhadra,
blew their conches—each and every one.

स घोषो धार्तराष्ट्राणां हृदयानि व्यदारयत् ।
नभश्च पृथिवीं चैव तुमुलो व्यनुनादयन् ॥ 19

This thundering sound rent the hearts of the sons of
Dhritarashtra, resounding through earth and sky.

अथ व्यवस्थितान्दृष्ट्वा धार्तराष्ट्रान्कपिध्वजः ।

प्रवृत्ते शस्त्रसंपाते धनुरुद्यम्य पाण्डवः ॥ 20
हृषीकेशं तदा वाक्यमिदमाह महीपते ।
सेनयोरुभयोर्मध्ये रथं स्थापय मेऽच्युत ॥ 21
यावदेतान्निरीक्षेऽहं योद्धुकामानवस्थितान् ।
कैर्मया सह योद्धव्यमस्मिन्रणसमुद्यमे ॥ 22

Then the ape-bannered son of Pandu, seeing the sons of Dhritarashtra lined up, lifted his bow as the clash of arms began and spoke these words to Hrishikesha, O Lord of the Earth: 'Achyuta, station my chariot between the two armies, so that I may observe these men, standing eager for battle, with whom I must fight in this strenuous engagement.

योत्स्यमानानवेक्षेऽहं य एतेऽत्र समागताः ।
धार्तराष्ट्रस्य दुर्बुद्धेर्युद्धे प्रियचिकीर्षवः ॥ 23

I see these men who have assembled here, ready to fight, wanting to please the evil-minded son of Dhritarashtra in battle.'

एवमुक्तो हृषीकेशो गुडाकेशेन भारत ।
सेनयोरुभयोर्मध्ये स्थापयित्वा रथोत्तमम् ॥ 24
भीष्मद्रोणप्रमुखतः सर्वेषां च महीक्षिताम् ।
उवाच पार्थ पश्यैतान्समवेतान्कुरूनिति ॥ 25

When Gudakesha had spoken to him thus, O Bharata, Hrishikesha stationed their splendid chariot between the two armies, right in front of Bhishma, Drona, and all the kings and said, 'Son of Pritha, behold these Kurus assembled.'

तत्रापश्यत्स्थितान्पार्थः पितॄनथ पितामहान् ।
आचार्यान्मातुलान्भ्रातॄन्पुत्रान्पौत्रान्सखींस्तथा ॥ 26
श्वशुरान्सुहृदश्चैव सेनयोरुभयोरपि ।
तान्समीक्ष्य स कौन्तेयः सर्वान्बन्धूनवस्थितान् ॥ 27
कृपया परयाविष्टो विषीदन्निदमब्रवीत् ।
दृष्ट्वेमान्स्वजनान्कृष्ण युयुत्सून्समवस्थितान् ॥ 28
सीदन्ति मम गात्राणि मुखं च परिशुष्यति ।
वेपथुश्च शरीरे मे रोमहर्षश्च जायते ॥ 29

There the son of Pritha saw standing fathers and grandfathers, as well as teachers, uncles, brothers, sons, grandsons, friends, fathers-in-law, and even allies in both armies. When the son of Kunti had seen them, all these relatives arrayed, he was overcome with the greatest compassion, deeply saddened, and said this: 'When I see my family willing and ready to fight, Krishna, my limbs falter, my mouth goes dry. There is a trembling in my body and my hairs bristle.

गाण्डीवं स्रंसते हस्तात्त्वक्चैव परिदह्यते ।
न च शक्नोम्यवस्थातुं भ्रमतीव च मे मनः ॥ 30

Gandiva slips from my hand, and as for my skin, it burns.
I cannot stand firm, and my mind seems to whirl.

निमित्तानि च पश्यामि विपरीतानि केशव ।
न च श्रेयोऽनुपश्यामि हत्वा स्वजनमाहवे ॥ 31

I see inauspicious portents, Keshava, and I see nothing good achieved by killing my family in battle.

न काङ्क्षे विजयं कृष्ण न च राज्यं सुखानि च ।
किं नो राज्येन गोविन्द किं भोगैर्जीवितेन वा ॥ 32

I don't desire victory, Krishna, nor a kingdom or pleasures.
What use is a kingdom to me, Govinda? What is enjoyment
or life?

येषामर्थे काङ्क्षितं नो राज्यं भोगाः सुखानि च ।
त इमेऽवस्थिता युद्धे प्राणांस्त्यक्त्वा धनानि च ॥ 33

For precisely those for whose sake we desire a kingdom,
enjoyment, and pleasures are standing in line to battle against
us, giving up their lives and riches.

आचार्याः पितरः पुत्रास्तथैव च पितामहाः ।
मातुलाः श्वशुराः पौत्राः स्यालाः संबन्धिनस्तथा ॥ 34
एतान्न हन्तुमिच्छामि घ्नतोऽपि मधुसूदन ।
अपि त्रैलोक्यराज्यस्य हेतोः किं नु महीकृते ॥ 35

Teachers, fathers, sons, yes, even grandfathers, uncles,
fathers-in-law, grandsons, brothers-in-law, and other
kinsmen—these I don't want to kill, even if they kill us,
Madhusudana, even for the kingdom of the three worlds,
and even less for the earth.

निहत्य धार्तराष्ट्रान्नः का प्रीतिः स्याज्जनार्दन ।
पापमेवाश्रयेदस्मान्हत्वैतानाततायिनः ॥ 36

What joy would we gain, Janardana, by killing the sons of
Dhritarashtra? Only evil would accrue to us by killing
these malefactors.

तस्मान्नार्हा वयं हन्तुं धार्तराष्ट्रान्सबान्धवान् ।
स्वजनं हि कथं हत्वा सुखिनः स्याम माधव ॥ 37

Therefore, we must not kill the sons of Dhritarashtra and our kinsmen. How could we become happy by killing our family?

यद्यप्येते न पश्यन्ति लोभोपहतचेतसः ।
कुलक्षयकृतं दोषं मित्रद्रोहे च पातकम् ॥ 38
कथं न ज्ञेयमस्माभिः पापादस्मान्निवर्तितुम् ।
कुलक्षयकृतं दोषं प्रपश्यद्भिर्जनार्दन ॥ 39

Even if they, their minds seduced by greed, do not see the wickedness of destroying the family and the crime in betraying their friends, how could we fail to know that we should turn away from this evil, we who see the wickedness of destroying the family, Janardana?

कुलक्षये प्रणश्यन्ति कुलधर्माः सनातनाः ।
धर्मे नष्टे कुलं कृत्स्नमधर्मोऽभिभवत्युत ॥ 40

When the family is destroyed, the eternal family laws are lost, and when the law is lost, lawlessness overwhelms the whole family.

अधर्माभिभवात्कृष्ण प्रदुष्यन्ति कुलस्त्रियः ।
स्त्रीषु दुष्टासु वार्ष्णेय जायते वर्णसंकरः ॥ 41
संकरो नरकायैव कुलघ्नानां कुलस्य च ।
पतन्ति पितरो ह्येषां लुप्तपिण्डोदकक्रियाः ॥ 42

Because lawlessness prevails, Krishna, the women of the family become corrupted. When the women are corrupted, Son of Vrishni, the classes get confused, a confusion leading to hell for family and family killers. For their fathers fall, deprived of their offerings of rice balls and water.

दोषैरेतैः कुलघ्नानां वर्णसंकरकारकैः ।
उत्साद्यन्ते जातिधर्माः कुलधर्माश्च शाश्वताः ॥ 43

Because of these transgressions of the family killers which cause confusion of the classes, the eternal caste laws and family laws are set aside.

उत्सन्नकुलधर्माणां मनुष्याणां जनार्दन ।
नरके नियतं वासो भवतीत्यनुशुश्रुम ॥ 44

We have heard, Janardana, that a place in hell is guaranteed for men who have set aside their family laws.

अहो बत महत्पापं कर्तुं व्यवसिता वयम् ।
यद्राज्यसुखलोभेन हन्तुं स्वजनमुद्यताः ॥ 45

Alas! We have decided to do great evil, because we are ready to kill our family out of greed for the pleasures of a kingdom.

यदि मामप्रतीकारमशस्त्रं शस्त्रपाणयः ।
धार्तराष्ट्रा रणे हन्युस्तन्मे क्षेमतरं भवेत् ॥ 46

If the sons of Dhritarashtra, weapons in hand, were to kill me in battle, unresisting and unarmed, that would be better for me.'

एवमुक्त्वार्जुनः संख्ये रथोपस्थ उपाविशत् ।
विसृज्य सशरं चापं शोकसंविग्नमानसः ॥ 47

With these words, Arjuna let go of his bow and arrows in
the midst of battle and sank down in his chariot, his mind
tormented by sorrow."

इति श्रीमहाभारते शतसाहस्रायां संहितायां श्रीमद्भगवद्गीतायां ब्रह्मविद्या-
शास्त्रे श्रीकृष्णार्जुनसंवादे अर्जुनविषादयोगो नाम प्रथमोऽध्यायः ॥

Thus ends the first chapter, entitled "The Reflection upon
Arjuna's Despair," in the instruction which teaches the sacred
knowledge given by the exalted Krishna in his conversation
with Arjuna, the auspicious Bhagavad Gita, which is in the
work of a hundred thousand verses, the glorious *Mahabharata*.

द्वितीयोऽध्यायः
Chapter Two

Theory

संजय उवाच ।
तं तथा कृपयाविष्टमश्रुपूर्णाकुलेक्षणम् ।
विषीदन्तमिदं वाक्यमुवाच मधुसूदनः ॥ 1

Sanjaya said, "Thus overcome with compassion, his eyes filled with tears in despair, Madhusudana spoke to him.

श्रीभगवानुवाच ।
कुतस्त्वा कश्मलमिदं विषमे समुपस्थितम् ।
अनार्यजुष्टमस्वर्ग्यमकीर्तिकरमर्जुन ॥ 2

The Lord said, 'Why has this foul delusion come over you in this critical hour, Arjuna? It is ignoble, it doesn't lead to heaven, and it is disgraceful.

क्लैब्यं मा स्म गमः पार्थ नैतत्त्वय्युपपद्यते ।
क्षुद्रं हृदयदौर्बल्यं त्यक्त्वोत्तिष्ठ परंतप ॥ 3

Do not succumb to cowardice, Son of Pritha. This is unworthy of you. Shake off this petty faintness of heart. Stand up, Scorcher of Enemies!'

अर्जुन उवाच ।
कथं भीष्ममहं संख्ये द्रोणं च मधुसूदन ।
इषुभिः प्रतियोत्स्यामि पूजार्हावरिसूदन ॥ 4

Arjuna said, 'How can I fight with arrows against Bhishma and Drona in battle, Madhusudana? They are worthy of homage, Enemy Slayer.

गुरूनहत्वा हि महानुभावाञ्श्रेयो भोक्तुं भैक्षमपीह लोके ।
हत्वार्थकामांस्तु गुरूनिहैव भुञ्जीय भोगानुधिरप्रदिग्धान् ॥ 5

It is better to eat beggars' food here in this world than to kill teachers of great honor. If I were to kill my teachers, who are greedy for wealth here, I would enjoy pleasures smeared with blood.

न चैतद्विद्मः कतरन्नो गरीयो यद्वा जयेम यदि वा नो जयेयुः ।
यानेव हत्वा न जिजीविषामस्तेऽवस्थिताः प्रमुखे धार्तराष्ट्राः ॥ 6

Nor do we know what is better for us, whether we win or lose. The sons of Dhritarashtra are arrayed before us. If we kill them, we shall not wish to live.

कार्पण्यदोषोपहतस्वभावः पृच्छामि त्वां धर्मसंमूढचेताः ।
यच्छ्रेयः स्यान्निश्चितं ब्रूहि तन्मे शिष्यस्तेऽहं शाधि मां त्वां प्रपन्नम् ॥ 7

My deepest nature has been stricken by the error of compassion. With a mind confused about the law, I ask you what would be best. Tell me this for sure. I am your student. Teach me as I seek refuge in you.

न हि प्रपश्यामि ममापनुद्याद्यच्छोकमुच्छोषणमिन्द्रियाणाम् ।
अवाप्य भूमावसपत्नमृद्धं राज्यं सुराणामपि चाधिपत्यम् ॥ 8

For I see nothing that would dispel this sorrow of mine which desiccates my senses, even if on earth I obtained unrivaled wealth, a kingdom, yes, even sovereignty over the gods!'"

संजय उवाच ।
एवमुक्त्वा हृषीकेशं गुडाकेशः परंतप ।
न योत्स्य इति गोविन्दमुक्त्वा तूष्णीं बभूव ह ॥ 9

Sanjaya said, "O Scorcher of Enemies, after Gudakesha said this to Hrishikesha, he added, 'I will not fight,' and then fell silent.

तमुवाच हृषीकेशः प्रहसन्निव भारत ।
सेनयोरुभयोर्मध्ये विषीदन्तमिदं वचः ॥ 10

With a hint of derision, O Bharata, Hrishikesha spoke these words to him as he sat despairing between the two armies.

श्रीभगवानुवाच ।
अशोच्यानन्वशोचस्त्वं प्रज्ञावादांश्च भाषसे ।
गतासूनगतासूंश्च नानुशोचन्ति पण्डिताः ॥ 11

The Lord said, 'You sorrow over men you should not be sorry for, yet you address issues of learning? Wise men grieve neither for the dead nor for the living.

न त्वेवाहं जातु नासं न त्वं नेमे जनाधिपाः ।
न चैव न भविष्यामः सर्वे वयमतः परम् ॥ 12

Never was there a time when I did not exist, nor you, nor these lords of men, and never shall any of us cease to exist hereafter.

देहिनोऽस्मिन्यथा देहे कौमारं यौवनं जरा ।
तथा देहान्तरप्राप्तिर्धीरस्तत्र न मुह्यति ॥ 13

Just as the embodied self passes through childhood, youth, and old age in this body, in the same manner, it will obtain another body. A wise man is not confused about this.

मात्रास्पर्शास्तु कौन्तेय शीतोष्णसुखदुःखदाः ।
आगमापायिनोऽनित्यास्तांस्तितिक्षस्व भारत ॥ 14

Contacts with the elements, Son of Kunti, are the source of cold, heat, pleasure, and pain. They come and go eternally. Endure them, Bharata!

यं हि न व्यथयन्त्येते पुरुषं पुरुषर्षभ ।
समदुःखसुखं धीरं सोऽमृतत्वाय कल्पते ॥ 15

The man whom they do not trouble, O Bull Among Men, the wise man for whom pain and pleasure are the same: He is fit for immortality.

नासतो विद्यते भावो नाभावो विद्यते सतः ।
उभयोरपि दृष्टोऽन्तस्त्वनयोस्तत्त्वदर्शिभिः ॥ 16

There is no becoming from the nonexistent, nor any unbecoming from the existent. The boundary between these two has been perceived by those who see the basic principles.

अविनाशि तु तद्विद्धि येन सर्वमिदं ततम् ।
विनाशमव्ययस्यास्य न कश्चित्कर्तुमर्हति ॥ 17

Know that this, on which all the world has been strung, is indestructible. No one can bring about the destruction of this imperishable being.

अन्तवन्त इमे देहा नित्यस्योक्ताः शरीरिणः ।
अनाशिनोऽप्रमेयस्य तस्माद्युध्यस्व भारत ॥ 18

It is these bodies of the embodied, eternal, imperishable, and unfathomable self which come to an end. Therefore fight, Bharata!

य एनं वेत्ति हन्तारं यश्चैनं मन्यते हतम् ।
उभौ तौ न विजानीतो नायं हन्ति न हन्यते ॥ 19

He who thinks the embodied self is a slayer, and he who imagines it is slain—neither of these understand. It does not slay, nor is it slain.

न जायते म्रियते वा कदाचिन्नायं भूत्वा भविता वा न भूयः ।
अजो नित्यः शाश्वतोऽयं पुराणो न हन्यते हन्यमाने शरीरे ॥ 20

It is never born and it never dies, nor will it come to life again when it has ceased to be. It is unborn, eternal, constant, and ancient. It is not slain when the body is slain.

वेदाविनाशिनं नित्यं य एनमजमव्ययम् ।
कथं स पुरुषः पार्थ कं घातयति हन्ति कम् ॥ 21

How does the man who knows this indestructible, eternal, unborn, and imperishable principle, Son of Pritha, have anybody killed, or kill anybody?

वासांसि जीर्णानि यथा विहाय नवानि गृह्णाति नरोऽपराणि ।
तथा शरीराणि विहाय जीर्णान्यन्यानि संयाति नवानि देही ॥ 22

Like a man who has cast off his old clothes puts on others that are new, thus the embodied self casts off old bodies and moves on to others that are new.

नैनं छिन्दन्ति शस्त्राणि नैनं दहति पावकः ।
न चैनं क्लेदयन्त्यापो न शोषयति मारुतः ॥ 23

Weapons do not cut it, fire does not burn it, water does not wet it, wind does not parch it.

अच्छेद्योऽयमदाह्योऽयमक्लेद्योऽशोष्य एव च ।
नित्यः सर्वगतः स्थाणुरचलोऽयं सनातनः ॥ 24

It cannot be cut, it cannot be burned, it cannot even be wetted or parched. It is eternal, omnipresent, firm, immovable, everlasting.

अव्यक्तोऽयमचिन्त्योऽयमविकार्योऽयमुच्यते ।
तस्मादेवं विदित्वैनं नानुशोचितुमर्हसि ॥ 25

It is unmanifest, it is inconceivable, it is said to be unchanging. Therefore, knowing it in this manner, do not mourn it.

अथ चैनं नित्यजातं नित्यं वा मन्यसे मृतम् ।
तथापि त्वं महाबाहो नैनं शोचितुमर्हसि ॥ 26

Even if you regard it as eternally born or eternally dead, you
still should not grieve over it, Mighty-armed Prince.

जातस्य हि ध्रुवो मृत्युर्ध्रुवं जन्म मृतस्य च ।
तस्मादपरिहार्येऽर्थे न त्वं शोचितुमर्हसि ॥ 27

For to the born, death is certain—and birth is certain to
the dead. Therefore, do not grieve over something that
is inescapable.

अव्यक्तादीनि भूतानि व्यक्तमध्यानि भारत ।
अव्यक्तनिधनान्येव तत्र का परिदेवना ॥ 28

The beginnings of beings are hidden, Bharata, their middle
periods are visible, and their ends are hidden again. What
reason is there to lament?

आश्चर्यवत्पश्यति कश्चिदेनमाश्चर्यवद्वदति तथैव चान्यः ।
आश्चर्यवच्चैनमन्यः शृणोति श्रुत्वाप्येनं वेद न चैव कश्चित् ॥ 29

Someone sees it as a miracle, another speaks of it as a miracle,
and yet another hears it as a miracle, but even if someone has
heard of it, no one really knows it.

देही नित्यमवध्योऽयं देहे सर्वस्य भारत ।
तस्मात्सर्वाणि भूतानि न त्वं शोचितुमर्हसि ॥ 30

This embodied self in anyone's body is always unslayable, Bharata. Therefore you should not grieve over any beings.

स्वधर्ममपि चावेक्ष्य न विकम्पितुमर्हसि ।
धर्म्याद्धि युद्धाच्छ्रेयोऽन्यत्क्षत्रियस्य न विद्यते ॥ 31

Yes, observe your personal law; do not waver. For there is nothing better for a warrior than lawful combat.

यदृच्छया चोपपन्नं स्वर्गद्वारमपावृतम् ।
सुखिनः क्षत्रियाः पार्थ लभन्ते युद्धमीदृशम् ॥ 32

And when it happens of its own accord, an open door to heaven, happy are the warriors, Son of Pritha, who obtain such combat.

अथ चेत्त्वमिमं धर्म्यं संग्रामं न करिष्यसि ।
ततः स्वधर्मं कीर्तिं च हित्वा पापमवाप्स्यसि ॥ 33

So, if you do not participate in this lawful battle, then you will give up your personal law and fame and incur guilt.

अकीर्तिं चापि भूतानि कथयिष्यन्ति तेऽव्ययाम् ।
संभावितस्य चाकीर्तिर्मरणादतिरिच्यते ॥ 34

The world will tell of your undying shame, and for the honored, shame is worse than death.

भयाद्रणादुपरतं मंस्यन्ते त्वां महारथाः ।
येषां च त्वं बहुमतो भूत्वा यास्यसि लाघवम् ॥ 35

The great warriors will think that you withdrew from battle out of fear, and you will lose the respect of those who held you in great esteem.

अवाच्यवादांश्च बहून्वदिष्यन्ति तवाहिताः ।
निन्दन्तस्तव सामर्थ्यं ततो दुःखतरं नु किम् ॥ 36

Your enemies will tell many unspeakable tales about you, mocking your strength. What could be worse than that?

हतो वा प्राप्स्यसि स्वर्गं जित्वा वा भोक्ष्यसे महीम् ।
तस्मादुत्तिष्ठ कौन्तेय युद्धाय कृतनिश्चयः ॥ 37

If you are killed, you will obtain heaven; if you are victorious, you will enjoy the earth. Therefore stand up, Son of Kunti, and resolve to battle!

सुखदुःखे समे कृत्वा लाभालाभौ जयाजयौ ।
ततो युद्धाय युज्यस्व नैवं पापमवाप्स्यसि ॥ 38

Treating happiness and unhappiness, profit and loss, victory and defeat alike, make yourself ready for battle! Thus you will incur no guilt.

एषा तेऽभिहिता सांख्ये बुद्धिर्योगे त्विमां शृणु ।
बुद्ध्या युक्तो यया पार्थ कर्मबन्धं प्रहास्यसि ॥ 39

This disposition has been explained to you in theory; now listen to it in practice. Endowed with this disposition, Son of Pritha, you will break the bonds of action.

नेहाभिक्रमनाशोऽस्ति प्रत्यवायो न विद्यते ।
स्वल्पमप्यस्य धर्मस्य त्रायते महतो भयात् ॥ ४०

There is no unsuccessful effort here, nor is there any backlash.
Even a little of this law saves one from great distress.

व्यवसायात्मिका बुद्धिरेकेह कुरुनन्दन ।
बहुशाखा ह्यनन्ताश्च बुद्धयोऽव्यवसायिनाम् ॥ ४१

In this there is a resolute disposition characterized by resolve,
Joy of the Kurus. But the minds of the irresolute are endless
and branch out in many directions.

यामिमां पुष्पितां वाचं प्रवदन्त्यविपश्चितः ।
वेदवादरताः पार्थ नान्यदस्तीति वादिनः ॥ ४२

This is the flowery language that the undiscerning use,
those who rejoice in Vedic discussions, Son of Pritha, saying,
"There is nothing else."

कामात्मानः स्वर्गपरा जन्मकर्मफलप्रदाम् ।
क्रियाविशेषबहुलां भोगैश्वर्यगतिं प्रति ॥ ४३

Their nature is desire, and they are set upon heaven. That
language gives rebirth as the fruit of actions, abounds in
many different rituals, and is aimed at obtaining pleasure
and power.

भोगैश्वर्यप्रसक्तानां तयापहृतचेतसाम् ।
व्यवसायात्मिका बुद्धिः समाधौ न विधीयते ॥ ४४

If the minds of such men are carried away by it, their intellectual concentration is not endowed with this resolute disposition because they are attached to pleasure and power.

त्रैगुण्यविषया वेदा निस्त्रैगुण्यो भवार्जुन ।
निर्द्वंद्वो नित्यसत्त्वस्थो निर्योगक्षेम आत्मवान् ॥ 45

The Vedas have the world of the triple properties as their subject. Stay aloof from this world of three qualities, Arjuna. Be indifferent to pairs of opposites, forever fixed in clarity, nonacquisitive, self-possessed.

यावानर्थ उदपाने सर्वतः संप्लुतोदके ।
तावान्सर्वेषु वेदेषु ब्राह्मणस्य विजानतः ॥ 46

As useful as a well when water is flooding everywhere, so are all the Vedas for an intelligent Brahmin.

कर्मण्येवाधिकारस्ते मा फलेषु कदाचन ।
मा कर्मफलहेतुर्भूर्मा ते सङ्गोऽस्त्वकर्मणि ॥ 47

You are only entitled to the action, never to its fruits. Do not let the fruits of action be your motive, but do not attach yourself to nonaction.

योगस्थः कुरु कर्माणि सङ्गं त्यक्त्वा धनंजय ।
सिद्ध्यसिद्ध्योः समो भूत्वा समत्वं योग उच्यते ॥ 48

Perform your actions with mental discipline, Dhananjaya, without attachment, remaining equable in success and failure. Equanimity is called Yoga.

दूरेण ह्यवरं कर्म बुद्धियोगाद्धनंजय ।
बुद्धौ शरणमन्विच्छ कृपणाः फलहेतवः ॥ 49

For action is by far inferior to a disciplined disposition, Dhananjaya. Seek shelter in your disposition! Miserable are those who are motivated by rewards.

बुद्धियुक्तो जहातीह उभे सुकृतदुष्कृते ।
तस्माद्योगाय युज्यस्व योगः कर्मसु कौशलम् ॥ 50

The man whose disposition is disciplined transcends both good and bad actions in this world. Therefore prepare yourself for Yoga. Yoga means great strength in actions.

कर्मजं बुद्धियुक्ता हि फलं त्यक्त्वा मनीषिणः ।
जन्मबन्धविनिर्मुक्ताः पदं गच्छन्त्यनामयम् ॥ 51

For men with disciplined minds wisely leave behind rewards born of action, and released from the bonds of birth, proceed to a stage free from sorrow.

यदा ते मोहकलिलं बुद्धिर्व्यतितरिष्यति ।
तदा गन्तासि निर्वेदं श्रोतव्यस्य श्रुतस्य च ॥ 52

When your mind crosses beyond the opacity of illusion, you will become indifferent to both future and past revelations.

श्रुतिविप्रतिपन्ना ते यदा स्थास्यति निश्चला ।
समाधावचला बुद्धिस्तदा योगमवाप्स्यसि ॥ 53

When your mind stands steady in disregard of revelation,
immovable in intellectual concentration, then you will achieve
mental discipline.'

अर्जुन उवाच ।
स्थितप्रज्ञस्य का भाषा समाधिस्थस्य केशव ।
स्थितधीः किं प्रभाषेत किमासीत व्रजेत किम् ॥ 54

Arjuna said, 'What is the definition of this man of steadfast
wisdom, standing in concentration, Keshava? How would this
steady-minded man speak, sit, and walk?'

श्रीभगवानुवाच ।
प्रजहाति यदा कामान्सर्वान्पार्थ मनोगतान् ।
आत्मन्येवात्मना तुष्टः स्थितप्रज्ञस्तदोच्यते ॥ 55

The Lord said, 'When a man, Son of Pritha, leaves behind
all desires that come to the mind, satisfied by and in himself,
then he is called a man of steadfast wisdom.

दुःखेष्वनुद्विग्नमनाः सुखेषु विगतस्पृहः ।
वीतरागभयक्रोधः स्थितधीर्मुनिरुच्यते ॥ 56

His mind is not ruffled in misfortune, he is without desire in
good fortune, his passion, fear, and anger have disappeared.
The steady-minded man is called a sage.

यः सर्वत्रानभिस्नेहस्तत्तत्प्राप्य शुभाशुभम् ।
नाभिनन्दति न द्वेष्टि तस्य प्रज्ञा प्रतिष्ठिता ॥ 57

He who is indifferent in all matters, who neither rejoices
nor hates whether he meets good or evil, his wisdom is
well founded.

यदा संहरते चायं कूर्मोऽङ्गानीव सर्वशः ।
इन्द्रियाणीन्द्रियार्थेभ्यस्तस्य प्रज्ञा प्रतिष्ठिता ॥ 58

And when he withdraws his senses from their objects, like a
tortoise retracting all its limbs, then his wisdom is well founded.

विषया विनिवर्तन्ते निराहारस्य देहिनः ।
रसवर्जं रसोऽप्यस्य परं दृष्ट्वा निवर्तते ॥ 59

Sense objects disappear for the embodied soul deprived of
food, except for their taste. Even the taste retreats when the
soul has seen the Supreme.

यततो ह्यपि कौन्तेय पुरुषस्य विपश्चितः ।
इन्द्रियाणि प्रमाथीनि हरन्ति प्रसभं मनः ॥ 60

For the exciting senses, Son of Kunti, forcibly steal the mind
of even a learned man who exerts himself.

तानि सर्वाणि संयम्य युक्त आसीत मत्परः ।
वशे हि यस्येन्द्रियाणि तस्य प्रज्ञा प्रतिष्ठिता ॥ 61

The disciplined man should bring them all under control and sit intent on me. For the wisdom of that man is well founded who has his senses in his power.

ध्यायतो विषयान्पुंसः सङ्गस्तेषूपजायते ।
सङ्गात्संजायते कामः कामात्क्रोधोऽभिजायते ॥ 62
क्रोधाद्भवति संमोहः संमोहात्स्मृतिविभ्रमः ।
स्मृतिभ्रंशाद्बुद्धिनाशो बुद्धिनाशात्प्रणश्यति ॥ 63

When a man contemplates sense objects, he grows attached to them. This attachment produces desire, and from desire, anger is born. Anger produces confusion, confusion produces loss of memory, loss of memory produces destruction of the mind, and because the mind is destroyed, he perishes.

रागद्वेषवियुक्तैस्तु विषयानिन्द्रियैश्चरन् ।
आत्मवश्यैर्विधेयात्मा प्रसादमधिगच्छति ॥ 64
प्रसादे सर्वदुःखानां हानिरस्योपजायते ।
प्रसन्नचेतसो ह्याशु बुद्धिः पर्यवतिष्ठते ॥ 65

But that man attains serenity whose self is obedient, who roams among the sense objects with his senses controlled by the self, untouched by passion and aversion. In a state of serenity, all sorrows disappear for him, for the mind of the man with a serene consciousness quickly becomes steady.

नास्ति बुद्धिरयुक्तस्य न चायुक्तस्य भावना ।
न चाभावयतः शान्तिरशान्तस्य कुतः सुखम् ॥ 66
इन्द्रियाणां हि चरतां यन्मनोऽनुविधीयते ।

तदस्य हरति प्रज्ञां वायुर्नाविमवाम्भसि ॥ 67

A man without mental discipline has no intelligence, nor any inclination for self-knowledge, nor is there tranquility for him who does not seek self-knowledge. How could the man bereft of tranquility find happiness? For when the mind yields to the roving senses, it carries away his wisdom like the wind carries away a boat on the water.

तस्माद्यस्य महाबाहो निगृहीतानि सर्वशः ।
इन्द्रियाणीन्द्रियार्थेभ्यस्तस्य प्रज्ञा प्रतिष्ठिता ॥ 68

Therefore, Mighty-armed Prince, the wisdom of that man whose senses are always withdrawn from the sense objects is well founded.

या निशा सर्वभूतानां तस्यां जागर्ति संयमी ।
यस्यां जाग्रति भूतानि सा निशा पश्यतो मुनेः ॥ 69

When it is night for all beings, the self-controlled man is awake. When the beings are awake, that is night for the seeing sage.

आपूर्यमाणमचलप्रतिष्ठं समुद्रमापः प्रविशन्ति यद्वत् ।
तद्वत्कामा यं प्रविशन्ति सर्वे स शान्तिमाप्नोति न कामकामी ॥ 70

That man attains tranquility into whom all desires flow like water flows into the sea and fills it without moving it, not he who is filled with desires.

विहाय कामान्यः सर्वान्पुमांश्चरति निःस्पृहः ।

निर्ममो निरहंकारः स शान्तिमधिगच्छति ॥ 71

The man who abandons all desires and roams about
without cravings, possessiveness, or ego-consciousness,
reaches tranquility.

एषा ब्राह्मी स्थितिः पार्थ नैनां प्राप्य विमुह्यति ।
स्थित्वास्यामन्तकालेऽपि ब्रह्मनिर्वाणमृच्छति ॥ 72

This is the Brahmic state, Son of Pritha! He who has obtained
it is not thrown into confusion. He who remains in it, even at
the moment of death, reaches the final emancipation.'

इति श्रीमहाभारते शतसाहस्रायां संहितायां श्रीमद्भगवद्गीतायां ब्रह्मविद्या-
शास्त्रे श्रीकृष्णार्जुनसंवादे सांख्ययोगो नाम द्वितीयोऽध्यायः ॥

Thus ends the second chapter, entitled "The Reflection
upon Theory," in the instruction which teaches the sacred
knowledge given by the exalted Krishna in his conversation
with Arjuna, the auspicious Bhagavad Gita, which is in the
work of a hundred thousand verses, the glorious *Mahabharata*.

तृतीयोऽध्यायः

Chapter Three

Action

अर्जुन उवाच ।
ज्यायसी चेत्कर्मणस्ते मता बुद्धिर्जनार्दन ।
तत्किं कर्मणि घोरे मां नियोजयसि केशव ॥ 1

Arjuna said, 'If you think, Janardana, that disposition is better than action, then why do you urge me to such terrible action, Keshava?

व्यामिश्रेणैव वाक्येन बुद्धिं मोहयसीव मे ।
तदेकं वद निश्चित्य येन श्रेयोऽहमाप्नुयाम् ॥ 2

It is as if you confuse my mind with self-contradictory words. So tell me unambiguously and definitively what I need to attain the supreme good.'

श्रीभगवानुवाच ।
लोकेऽस्मिन्द्विविधा निष्ठा पुरा प्रोक्ता मयानघ ।
ज्ञानयोगेन सांख्यानां कर्मयोगेन योगिनाम् ॥ 3

The Lord said, 'In this world, I have formerly taught two alternatives, blameless Prince: the discipline of knowledge for men of intellect, and the discipline of action for men of action.

न कर्मणामनारम्भान्नैष्कर्म्यं पुरुषोऽश्नुते ।
न च संन्यसनादेव सिद्धिं समधिगच्छति ॥ ४

A man does not avoid karma because he ceases to undertake actions, nor does he fully reach success simply by renunciation.

न हि कश्चित्क्षणमपि जातु तिष्ठत्यकर्मकृत् ।
कार्यते ह्यवशः कर्म सर्वः प्रकृतिजैर्गुणैः ॥ ५

Indeed, no one remains without acting even for a moment. For everybody is made to act willy-nilly by the three properties produced by primordial nature.

कर्मेन्द्रियाणि संयम्य य आस्ते मनसा स्मरन् ।
इन्द्रियार्थान्विमूढात्मा मिथ्याचारः स उच्यते ॥ ६

He who controls his organs of action, but sits brooding over sense objects in his mind like a deluded soul, he is called a hypocrite.

यस्त्विन्द्रियाणि मनसा नियम्यारभतेऽर्जुन ।
कर्मेन्द्रियैः कर्मयोगमसक्तः स विशिष्यते ॥ ७

But he who, controlling his senses with his mind, Arjuna, undertakes the discipline of action with his organs of action, he is distinguished as a man detached from worldly passions.

नियतं कुरु कर्म त्वं कर्म ज्यायो ह्यकर्मणः ।
शरीरयात्रापि च ते न प्रसिध्येदकर्मणः ॥ ८

You must perform a customary action, for that is better than inaction. Even the mere maintenance of your body would not succeed without actions.

यज्ञार्थात्कर्मणोऽन्यत्र लोकोऽयं कर्मबन्धनः ।
तदर्थं कर्म कौन्तेय मुक्तसङ्गः समाचर ॥ ९

With the exception of action done for the sake of sacrifice, this world is bound by the consequences of action. Therefore, Son of Kunti, perform actions free from attachment.

सहयज्ञाः प्रजाः सृष्ट्वा पुरोवाच प्रजापतिः ।
अनेन प्रसविष्यध्वमेष वोऽस्त्विष्टकामधुक् ॥ १०

When Prajapati in ancient times had brought forth creatures and the sacrifice, he said, "With this you shall procreate, this shall be the Cow of Plenty for your desires."

देवान्भावयतानेन ते देवा भावयन्तु वः ।
परस्परं भावयन्तः श्रेयः परमवाप्स्यथ ॥ ११

Strengthen the gods with it, let the gods strengthen you. When you strengthen each other, you will obtain the ultimate good.

इष्टान्भोगान्हि वो देवा दास्यन्ते यज्ञभाविताः ।
तैर्दत्तानप्रदायैभ्यो यो भुङ्क्ते स्तेन एव सः ॥ १२

The gods will give you the enjoyments you desire when they are strengthened by sacrifice. The man who enjoys gifts from them without giving them anything in return is simply a thief.

यज्ञशिष्टाशिनः सन्तो मुच्यन्ते सर्वकिल्बिषैः ।
भुञ्जते ते त्वघं पापा ये पचन्त्यात्मकारणात् ॥ 13

Those who eat the remains of sacrifices will be released from all sins. But the wicked who only cook for themselves eat filth.

अन्नाद्भवन्ति भूतानि पर्जन्यादन्नसंभवः ।
यज्ञाद्भवति पर्जन्यो यज्ञः कर्मसमुद्भवः ॥ 14

Beings spring from food, food springs from rain, rain springs from sacrifice, and sacrifice springs from action.

कर्म ब्रह्मोद्भवं विद्धि ब्रह्माक्षरसमुद्भवम् ।
तस्मात्सर्वगतं ब्रह्म नित्यं यज्ञे प्रतिष्ठितम् ॥ 15

Know that action springs from Brahman, and that Brahman springs from the immutable.

एवं प्रवर्तितं चक्रं नानुवर्तयतीह यः ।
अघायुरिन्द्रियारामो मोघं पार्थ स जीवति ॥ 16

Thus set in motion, he who does not keep the wheel turning in this world, Son of Pritha, lives a malicious life in vain, indulging his senses.

यस्त्वात्मरतिरेव स्यादात्मतृप्तश्च मानवः ।

आत्मन्येव च संतुष्टस्तस्य कार्यं न विद्यते ॥ 17

But the man who delights in the self alone, who is satiated
with the self, and who is deeply contented with nothing but
the self, he has no work to do.

नैव तस्य कृतेनार्थो नाकृतेनेह कश्चन ।
न चास्य सर्वभूतेषु कश्चिदर्थव्यपाश्रयः ॥ 18

He has nothing at all to gain from actions performed or not
performed, nor does he have any vested interest in anything.

तस्मादसक्तः सततं कार्यं कर्म समाचर ।
असक्तो ह्याचरन्कर्म परमाप्नोति पूरुषः ॥ 19

Therefore, you should always perform actions that have to be
done disinterestedly, for a man who performs acts disinterestedly reaches the supreme good.

कर्मणैव हि संसिद्धिमास्थिता जनकादयः ।
लोकसंग्रहमेवापि संपश्यन्कर्तुमर्हसि ॥ 20

Kings like Janaka achieved success precisely by action.
You should definitely act with a view to keeping the world
on course.

यद्यदाचरति श्रेष्ठस्तत्तदेवेतरो जनः ।
स यत्प्रमाणं कुरुते लोकस्तदनुवर्तते ॥ 21

Whatever the best man does, the other men do as well. People
follow the standard he sets.

न मे पार्थास्ति कर्तव्यं त्रिषु लोकेषु किंचन ।
नानवाप्तमवाप्तव्यं वर्त एव च कर्मणि ॥ 22

I do not have to do anything at all in the three worlds, Son of
Pritha, nor obtain anything that has not been obtained. Yet I
engage in action.

यदि ह्यहं न वर्तेयं जातु कर्मण्यतन्द्रितः ।
मम वर्त्मानुवर्तन्ते मनुष्याः पार्थ सर्वशः ॥ 23

For if I, unwearied, were not to engage in action, men would
follow my example in every way.

उत्सीदेयुरिमे लोका न कुर्यां कर्म चेदहम् ।
संकरस्य च कर्ता स्यामुपहन्यामिमाः प्रजाः ॥ 24

These worlds would collapse if I did not act, and I would create
confusion amongst the castes. I would destroy these people.

सक्ताः कर्मण्यविद्वांसो यथा कुर्वन्ति भारत ।
कुर्याद्विद्वांस्तथासक्तश्चिकीर्षुर्लोकसंग्रहम् ॥ 25

The learned man should act in the same way as an ignorant
man who is attached to action, Bharata, but without attachment, in order to keep the world on its course.

न बुद्धिभेदं जनयेदज्ञानां कर्मसङ्गिनाम् ।
जोषयेत्सर्वकर्माणि विद्वान्युक्तः समाचरन् ॥ 26

The learned man should not unsettle the minds of the
ignorant who are attached to action. He should take pleasure
in all actions, but perform them in a disciplined manner.

प्रकृतेः क्रियमाणानि गुणैः कर्माणि सर्वशः ।
अहंकारविमूढात्मा कर्ताहमिति मन्यते ॥ 27

Actions are universally performed by the properties of
primordial nature. The one whose self is deluded by
ego-consciousness thinks, "I am acting."

तत्त्ववित्तु महाबाहो गुणकर्मविभागयोः ।
गुणा गुणेषु वर्तन्त इति मत्वा न सज्जते ॥ 28

The man who knows the truth, Mighty-armed Prince,
about the distributions of those properties and their actions
does not get attached, knowing that properties are interacting
with properties.

प्रकृतेर्गुणसंमूढाः सज्जन्ते गुणकर्मसु ।
तानकृत्स्नविदो मन्दान्कृत्स्नविन्न विचालयेत् ॥ 29

Those who are deluded by the properties of primordial
nature get attached to the actions of the properties. But let
no man who knows the whole upset the slow-witted who are
ignorant of it.

मयि सर्वाणि कर्माणि संन्यस्याध्यात्मचेतसा ।
निराशीर्निर्ममो भूत्वा युध्यस्व विगतज्वरः ॥ 30

With your mind fixed on the supreme self, surrender all actions to me, shun desires and selfishness, and fight without remorse.

ये मे मतमिदं नित्यमनुतिष्ठन्ति मानवाः ।
श्रद्धावन्तोऽनसूयन्तो मुच्यन्ते तेऽपि कर्मभिः ॥ 31

Those who practice this eternal doctrine of mine full of faith and without grumbling are released from their actions.

ये त्वेतदभ्यसूयन्तो नानुतिष्ठन्ति मे मतम् ।
सर्वज्ञानविमूढांस्तान्विद्धि नष्टानचेतसः ॥ 32

But those who grumble and don't practice my doctrine, those you should know are deluded in all their knowledge, lost and witless.

सदृशं चेष्टते स्वस्याः प्रकृतेर्ज्ञानवानपि ।
प्रकृतिं यान्ति भूतानि निग्रहः किं करिष्यति ॥ 33

Even the man of knowledge acts in accordance with his own nature. All beings follow their nature—what will suppress them?

इन्द्रियस्येन्द्रियस्यार्थे रागद्वेषौ व्यवस्थितौ ।
तयोर्न वशमागच्छेत्तौ ह्यस्य परिपन्थिनौ ॥ 34

Love and hatred are lurking in the object of every single sense. A man should not fall into their power, for they will ambush him.

श्रेयान्स्वधर्मो विगुणः परधर्मात्स्वनुष्ठितात् ।
स्वधर्मे निधनं श्रेयः परधर्मो भयावहः ॥ 35

It is better to carry out one's own duty imperfectly, than another's duty well. It is better to die following one's own duty—another's duty is perilous.'

अर्जुन उवाच ।
अथ केन प्रयुक्तोऽयं पापं चरति पूरुषः ।
अनिच्छन्नपि वार्ष्णेय बलादिव नियोजितः ॥ 36

Arjuna said, 'So what is it that makes a man do evil, even unwillingly, Son of Vrishni, as if compelled by force?'

श्रीभगवानुवाच ।
काम एष क्रोध एष रजोगुणसमुद्भवः ।
महाशनो महापाप्मा विद्ध्येनमिह वैरिणम् ॥ 37

The Lord said, 'That is desire, that is anger produced by the property of agitation, the great devourer, the great evil. Know that this is the enemy in this world.

धूमेनाव्रियते वह्निर्यथादर्शो मलेन च ।
यथोल्बेनावृतो गर्भस्तथा तेनेदमावृतम् ॥ 38

As fire is clouded by smoke and a mirror by dust, as the embryo is coated by the caul, thus this world is darkened by agitation.

आवृतं ज्ञानमेतेन ज्ञानिनो नित्यवैरिणा ।

कामरूपेण कौन्तेय दुष्पूरेणानलेन च ॥ 39

This eternal enemy of the sage, Son of Kunti, envelopes
knowledge in the shape of desire, an insatiable fire.

इन्द्रियाणि मनो बुद्धिरस्याधिष्ठानमुच्यते ।
एतैर्विमोहयत्येष ज्ञानमावृत्य देहिनम् ॥ 40

Its foundation is said to be the senses, the mind, and the
intellect. Through these, it obscures knowledge and confuses
the embodied self.

तस्मात्त्वमिन्द्रियाण्यादौ नियम्य भरतर्षभ ।
पाप्मानं प्रजहिह्येनं ज्ञानविज्ञाननाशनम् ॥ 41

Therefore you should first control your senses, Bull of the
Bharatas, and slay this evil that destroys your knowledge
and discrimination.

इन्द्रियाणि पराण्याहुरिन्द्रियेभ्यः परं मनः ।
मनसस्तु परा बुद्धिर्यो बुद्धेः परतस्तु सः ॥ 42

They say that the senses are great. Greater than the senses is
the mind, greater than the mind is the intellect, but greater
than the intellect is the self.

एवं बुद्धेः परं बुट्ध्वा संस्तभ्यात्मानमात्मना ।
जहि शत्रुं महाबाहो कामरूपं दुरासदम् ॥ 43

When you have thus understood what is greater than the
intellect, when you have strengthened your self by your self,

Mighty-armed Prince, kill the enemy, so hard to assail, which
has the form of desire.'

इति श्रीमहाभारते शतसाहस्रायां संहितायां श्रीमद्भगवद्गीतायां
ब्रह्मविद्याशास्त्रे श्रीकृष्णार्जुनसंवादे कर्मयोगो नाम तृतीयोऽध्यायः ॥

Thus ends the third chapter, entitled "The Reflection
upon Action," in the instruction which teaches the sacred
knowledge given by the exalted Krishna in his conversation
with Arjuna, the auspicious Bhagavad Gita, which is in the
work of a hundred thousand verses, the glorious *Mahabharata*.

Knowledge, Action
and Renunciation

श्रीभगवानुवाच ।
इमं विवस्वते योगं प्रोक्तवानहमव्ययम् ।
विवस्वान्मनवे प्राह मनुरिक्ष्वाकवेऽब्रवीत् ॥ 1

The Lord said, 'I proclaimed this imperishable Yoga to
Vivasvat, Vivasvat announced it to Manu, and Manu told
it to Ikshvaku.

एवं परंपराप्राप्तमिमं राजर्षयो विदुः ।
स कालेनेह महता योगो नष्टः परंतप ॥ 2

Thus the royal sages knew it as handed down by tradition. But
here on earth, this Yoga has been lost, Scorcher of Enemies,
through the long lapse of time.

स एवायं मया तेऽद्य योगः प्रोक्तः पुरातनः ।
भक्तोऽसि मे सखा चेति रहस्यं ह्येतदुत्तमम् ॥ 3

It is precisely this ancient Yoga that I have proclaimed to you today because you are my devotee and my friend, for this is the ultimate mystery.'

अर्जुन उवाच ।
अपरं भवतो जन्म परं जन्म विवस्वतः ।
कथमेतद्विजानीयां त्वमादौ प्रोक्तवानिति ॥ ४

Arjuna said, 'But your birth was later than the birth of Vivasvat. How should I understand the fact that you spoke to him in the beginning?'

श्रीभगवानुवाच ।
बहूनि मे व्यतीतानि जन्मानि तव चार्जुन ।
तान्यहं वेद सर्वाणि न त्वं वेत्थ परंतप ॥ ५

The Lord said, 'Both you and I, Arjuna, have had many births in the past. I know them all; you do not know them, Scorcher of Enemies.

अजोऽपि सन्नव्ययात्मा भूतानामीश्वरोऽपि सन् ।
प्रकृतिं स्वामधिष्ठाय संभवाम्यात्ममायया ॥ ६

Although I am unborn, have an eternal self, and am the lord of beings, I am born through my own wizardry, by resorting to my own primordial nature.

यदा यदा हि धर्मस्य ग्लानिर्भवति भारत ।
अभ्युत्थानमधर्मस्य तदात्मानं सृजाम्यहम् ॥ ७

For whenever the law declines and lawlessness is on the rise, Bharata, then I create myself.

परित्राणाय साधूनां विनाशाय च दुष्कृताम् ।
धर्मसंस्थापनार्थाय संभवामि युगे युगे ॥ ८

I am born from age to age to protect the good and destroy the wicked in order to establish the law.

जन्म कर्म च मे दिव्यमेवं यो वेत्ति तत्त्वतः ।
त्यक्त्वा देहं पुनर्जन्म नैति मामेति सोऽर्जुन ॥ ९

Thus one who is truly conversant with the divine nature of my birth and actions is not born again, Arjuna. When he leaves his body, he comes to me.

वीतरागभयक्रोधा मन्मया मामुपाश्रिताः ।
बहवो ज्ञानतपसा पूता मद्भावमागताः ॥ १०

Delivered from passion, fear, and anger; absorbed in me, resorting to me—many purified by the austerity of knowledge reached my state of being.

ये यथा मां प्रपद्यन्ते तांस्तथैव भजाम्यहम् ।
मम वर्त्मानुवर्तन्ते मनुष्याः पार्थ सर्वशः ॥ ११

I accept men in precisely the same manner as they seek refuge in me. Men follow my lead in their various ways, Son of Pritha.

काङ्क्षन्तः कर्मणां सिद्धिं यजन्त इह देवताः ।

क्षिप्रं हि मानुषे लोके सिद्धिर्भवति कर्मजा ॥ 12

Those who want their actions to succeed sacrifice to the gods in this world. For in the world of men, success is quickly born of action.

चातुर्वर्ण्यं मया सृष्टं गुणकर्मविभागशः ।
तस्य कर्तारमपि मां विद्ध्यकर्तारमव्ययम् ॥ 13

I brought forth the four-class system according to the division of properties and actions. You should know that, although I am its maker, I am eternally inactive.

न मां कर्माणि लिम्पन्ति न मे कर्मफले स्पृहा ।
इति मां योऽभिजानाति कर्मभिर्न स बध्यते ॥ 14

Actions do not defile me; I have no yearning for their fruits. He who knows me in this way is not bound by his actions.

एवं ज्ञात्वा कृतं कर्म पूर्वैरपि मुमुक्षुभिः ।
कुरु कर्मैव तस्मात्त्वं पूर्वैः पूर्वतरं कृतम् ॥ 15

Knowing this, those who sought release even in ancient times performed actions. Therefore, you should do as it was done by the ancients long ago.

किं कर्म किमकर्मेति कवयोऽप्यत्र मोहिताः ।
तत्ते कर्म प्रवक्ष्यामि यज्ज्ञात्वा मोक्ष्यसेऽशुभात् ॥ 16

Even wise men are confused about what action and inaction are. I will therefore explain action to you. Knowing that, you will be released from evil.

कर्मणो ह्यपि बोद्धव्यं बोद्धव्यं च विकर्मणः ।
अकर्मणश्च बोद्धव्यं गहना कर्मणो गतिः ॥ 17

For one should know about action, know about misaction, and know about inaction. The course of action is hard to understand.

कर्मण्यकर्म यः पश्येदकर्मणि च कर्म यः ।
स बुद्धिमान्मनुष्येषु स युक्तः कृत्स्नकर्मकृत् । 18

If he were to see inaction in action, and action in inaction, he would be wise among men. He would be mentally disciplined when performing all actions.

यस्य सर्वे समारम्भाः कामसंकल्पवर्जिताः ।
ज्ञानाग्निदग्धकर्माणं तमाहुः पण्डितं बुधाः ॥ 19

The wise call him a learned man whose enterprises are all devoid of the intentions produced by desire. His actions have burned up in the fire of knowledge.

त्यक्त्वा कर्मफलासङ्गं नित्यतृप्तो निराश्रयः ।
कर्मण्यभिप्रवृत्तोऽपि नैव किंचित्करोति सः ॥ 20

Having given up attachment to the fruits of action, forever content and independent, he does not act at all—even when he is engaged in action.

निराशीर्यतचित्तात्मा त्यक्तसर्वपरिग्रहः ।
शारीरं केवलं कर्म कुर्वन्नाप्नोति किल्बिषम् ॥ 21

Without expectations, with mind and self under control, renouncing all possessions, he only performs bodily actions and does not suffer any guilt.

यदृच्छालाभसंतुष्टो द्वंद्वातीतो विमत्सरः ।
समः सिद्धावसिद्धौ च कृत्वापि न निबध्यते ॥ 22

He who is satisfied with whatever comes by chance, has risen above the pairs of opposites, is free from envy, and is equable in success and failure, he is not bound, even if he acts.

गतसङ्गस्य मुक्तस्य ज्ञानावस्थितचेतसः ।
यज्ञायाचरतः कर्म समग्रं प्रविलीयते ॥ 23

The action of a man whose attachment is gone, who is released, whose mind is founded on knowledge, and who acts for sacrificial reasons, is dissolved entirely.

ब्रह्मार्पणं ब्रह्महविर्ब्रह्माग्नौ ब्रह्मणा हुतम् ।
ब्रह्मैव तेन गन्तव्यं ब्रह्मकर्मसमाधिना ॥ 24

Brahman is the offering, Brahman is the oblation, Brahman is poured by Brahman into the fire. It is to Brahman he must go, he who contemplates action as Brahman.

दैवमेवापरे यज्ञं योगिनः पर्युपासते ।
ब्रह्माग्नावपरे यज्ञं यज्ञेनैवोपजुह्वति ॥ 25

Some yogis offer sacrifice to the gods, others pour the sacrifice into the fire of Brahman by means of the sacrifice.

श्रोत्रादीनीन्द्रियाण्यन्ये संयमाग्निषु जुह्वति ।
शब्दादीन्विषयानन्य इन्द्रियाग्निषु जुह्वति ॥ 26

Others offer their hearing and other senses into the fires of self-control, yet others offer sounds and other objects of the senses into the fires of the senses.

सर्वाणीन्द्रियकर्माणि प्राणकर्माणि चापरे ।
आत्मसंयमयोगाग्नौ जुह्वति ज्ञानदीपिते ॥ 27

Still others offer all sense actions, and actions of the vital breath, into the fire of self-control and the Yoga kindled by knowledge.

द्रव्ययज्ञास्तपोयज्ञा योगयज्ञास्तथापरे ।
स्वाध्यायज्ञानयज्ञाश्च यतयः संशितव्रताः ॥ 28

In the same manner, other devotees of strict vows sacrifice with their material wealth, their austerity, their Yoga, or their Vedic study and knowledge.

अपाने जुह्वति प्राणं प्राणेऽपानं तथापरे ।
प्राणापानगती रुद्ध्वा प्राणायामपरायणाः ॥ 29

Others again offer their inhaled breath into their exhaled breath, and their exhaled breath into their inhaled breath, by blocking the passages of the inhaled and exhaled breath with the aim of controlling their breathing.

अपरे नियताहाराः प्राणान्प्राणेषु जुह्वति ।
सर्वेऽप्येते यज्ञविदो यज्ञक्षपितकल्मषाः ॥ 30

Others, eating little, offer their inhaled breaths into their inhaled breaths. All these are sacrificial experts whose moral stains are destroyed by sacrifice.

यज्ञशिष्टामृतभुजो यान्ति ब्रह्म सनातनम् ।
नायं लोकोऽस्त्ययज्ञस्य कुतोऽन्यः कुरुसत्तम ॥ 31

Those who eat the remains of the sacrifice go to the eternal Brahman. This is not a world for those who do not sacrifice; how then any other world, Best of the Kurus?

एवं बहुविधा यज्ञा वितता ब्रह्मणो मुखे ।
कर्मजान्विद्धि तान्सर्वानेवं ज्ञात्वा विमोक्ष्यसे ॥ 32

Thus, sacrifices of many kinds are spread out in the mouth of Brahman. Know that all these experts on action will be released through this knowledge.

श्रेयान्द्रव्यमयाद्यज्ञाज्ज्ञानयज्ञः परंतप ।

सर्वं कर्माखिलं पार्थ ज्ञाने परिसमाप्यते ॥ 33

Better than a sacrifice of material wealth is a sacrifice of
knowledge, Scorcher of Enemies. All action without exception,
Son of Pritha, culminates in knowledge.

तद्विद्धि प्रणिपातेन परिप्रश्नेन सेवया ।
उपदेक्ष्यन्ति ते ज्ञानं ज्ञानिनस्तत्त्वदर्शिनः ॥ 34

Therefore, know that the sages who see the truth will show
you the knowledge, due to your obeisance, inquiry, and service.

यज्ज्ञात्वा न पुनर्मोहमेवं यास्यसि पाण्डव ।
येन भूतान्यशेषेण द्रक्ष्यस्यात्मन्यथो मयि ॥ 35

With this knowledge, Son of Pandu, you will no more become
confused! Through this, you will see all beings, without
exception, within your self, and then within me.

अपि चेदसि पापेभ्यः सर्वेभ्यः पापकृत्तमः ।
सर्वं ज्ञानप्लवेनैव वृजिनं संतरिष्यसि ॥ 36

Even if you are the greatest evil-doer of all sinners, you
will cross over all wickedness simply by using the boat
of knowledge.

यथैधांसि समिद्धोऽग्निर्भस्मसात्कुरुतेऽर्जुन ।
ज्ञानाग्निः सर्वकर्माणि भस्मसात्कुरुते तथा ॥ 37

As a kindled fire burns its fuel to ashes, Arjuna, thus the fire
of knowledge burns all actions to ashes.

न हि ज्ञानेन सदृशं पवित्रमिह विद्यते ।
तत्स्वयं योगसंसिद्धः कालेनात्मनि विन्दति ॥ 38

For there is no purifier in this world like knowledge. With
time, the man perfected in Yoga finds this of himself
in himself.

श्रद्धावाँल्लभते ज्ञानं तत्परः संयतेन्द्रियः ।
ज्ञानं लब्ध्वा परां शान्तिमचिरेणाधिगच्छति ॥ 39

The man of faith gains knowledge when he is devoted to it
and has his senses under control. Having gained knowledge,
he quickly reaches supreme peace.

अज्ञश्चाश्रद्दधानश्च संशयात्मा विनश्यति ।
नायं लोकोऽस्ति न परो न सुखं संशयात्मनः ॥ 40

The ignorant man of no faith, with a doubting soul, perishes.
There is neither this world or the next, nor any happiness for
the man with a doubting soul.

योगसंन्यस्तकर्माणं ज्ञानसंछिन्नसंशयम् ।
आत्मवन्तं न कर्माणि निबध्नन्ति धनंजय ॥ 41

Actions do not bind the man who has renounced actions
through Yoga, who has destroyed his doubts with knowledge,
and who has mastered himself, Dhananjaya.

तस्मादज्ञानसंभूतं हृत्स्थं ज्ञानासिनात्मनः ।
छित्त्वैनं संशयं योगमातिष्ठोत्तिष्ठ भारत ॥ 42

So hack away this doubt in your heart, springing from ignorance, with the sword of knowledge! Rely on Yoga, Bharata! Arise!'

इति श्रीमहाभारते शतसाहस्रायां संहितायां श्रीमद्भगवद्गीतायां ब्रह्मविद्या-
शास्त्रे श्रीकृष्णार्जुनसंवादे ज्ञानकर्मसंन्यासयोगो नाम चतुर्थोऽध्यायः ॥

Thus ends the fourth chapter, entitled "The Reflection upon Knowledge, Action, and Renunciation," in the instruction which teaches the sacred knowledge given by the exalted Krishna in his conversation with Arjuna, the auspicious Bhagavad Gita, which is in the work of a hundred thousand verses, the glorious *Mahabharata*.

पञ्चमोऽध्यायः

Chapter Five

Renunciation

अर्जुन उवाच ।
संन्यासं कर्मणां कृष्ण पुनर्योगं च शंससि ।
यच्छ्रेय एतयोरेकं तन्मे ब्रूहि सुनिश्चितम् ॥ 1

Arjuna said, 'You praise renunciation of actions and at the same time their performance, Krishna. Tell me for certain which is the better of these two.'

श्रीभगवानुवाच ।
संन्यासः कर्मयोगश्च निःश्रेयसकरावुभौ ।
तयोस्तु कर्मसंन्यासात्कर्मयोगो विशिष्यते ॥ 2

The Lord said, 'Both renunciation and performance of actions lead to ultimate bliss. But of these, performance of actions is better than renunciation of actions.

ज्ञेयः स नित्यसंन्यासी यो न द्वेष्टि न काङ्क्षति ।
निर्द्वन्द्वो हि महाबाहो सुखं बन्धात्प्रमुच्यते ॥ 3

He who neither hates nor desires should be known as an eternal renouncer. For the man who is indifferent to the pairs of opposites, Mighty-armed Prince, is easily released from bondage.

सांख्ययोगौ पृथग्बालाः प्रवदन्ति न पण्डिताः ।
एकमप्यास्थितः सम्यगुभयोर्विन्दते फलम् ॥ 4

The foolish say that theory and practice are different things—not men of learning. Even if a man only relies on one of these, he gets the full fruit of both.

यत्सांख्यैः प्राप्यते स्थानं तद्योगैरपि गम्यते ।
एकं सांख्यं च योगं च यः पश्यति स पश्यति ॥ 5

The goal obtained by men of intellect is also reached by men of action. He who sees that theory and practice are one has true insight.

संन्यासस्तु महाबाहो दुःखमाप्तुमयोगतः ।
योगयुक्तो मुनिर्ब्रह्म नचिरेणाधिगच्छति ॥ 6

But, Mighty-armed Prince, renunciation is difficult to accomplish without Yoga. The sage with mental discipline soon reaches Brahman.

योगयुक्तो विशुद्धात्मा विजितात्मा जितेन्द्रियः ।
सर्वभूतात्मभूतात्मा कुर्वन्नपि न लिप्यते ॥ 7

The man equipped with mental discipline, with a pure self, who has conquered the self as well as the senses, and whose self has become the self of all beings, is not tainted even if he acts.

नैव किंचित्करोमीति युक्तो मन्येत तत्त्ववित् ।
पश्यञ्शृण्वन्स्पृशञ्जिघ्रन्नश्नन्गच्छन्स्वपञ्श्वसन् ॥ 8
प्रलपन्विसृजन्गृह्णन्नुन्मिषन्निमिषन्नपि ।
इन्द्रियाणीन्द्रियार्थेषु वर्तन्त इति धारयन् ॥ 9

The mentally disciplined knower of truth should think, "I do not do anything," even when he sees, hears, touches, smells, walks, sleeps, breathes, talks, defecates, grasps, and opens and closes his eyes, realizing that this is the senses operating on their sense objects.

ब्रह्मण्याधाय कर्माणि सङ्गं त्यक्त्वा करोति यः ।
लिप्यते न स पापेन पद्मपत्रमिवाम्भसा ॥ 10

He who acts while resigning his actions to Brahman and giving up attachment is untainted by evil, just like the lotus leaf is untainted by water.

कायेन मनसा बुद्ध्या केवलैरिन्द्रियैरपि ।
योगिनः कर्म कुर्वन्ति सङ्गं त्यक्त्वात्मशुद्धये ॥ 11

Yogis perform actions with their body, mind, intellect, even with their senses, renouncing attachment to purify the self.

युक्तः कर्मफलं त्यक्त्वा शान्तिमाप्नोति नैष्ठिकीम् ।
अयुक्तः कामकारेण फले सक्तो निबध्यते ॥ 12

The mentally disciplined achieves final peace by renouncing the fruits of action. The undisciplined acting on his desires is fettered because he is attached to the fruit.

सर्वकर्माणि मनसा संन्यस्यास्ते सुखं वशी ।
नवद्वारे पुरे देही नैव कुर्वन्न कारयन् ॥ 13

Renouncing all actions with its mind, the self in the body
(the fortress of nine gates) remains at ease, in control of itself,
neither acting nor causing actions.

न कर्तृत्वं न कर्माणि लोकस्य सृजति प्रभुः ।
न कर्मफलसंयोगं स्वभावस्तु प्रवर्तते ॥ 14

The lord of the world neither creates agency nor actions, nor
the association between the actions and their fruit. That is
rather the work of primordial nature inherent in him.

नादत्ते कस्यचित्पापं न चैव सुकृतं विभुः ।
अज्ञानेनावृतं ज्ञानं तेन मुह्यन्ति जन्तवः ॥ 15

The lord does not take on anybody's crime or merit.
Knowledge is clouded by ignorance, therefore people
are confused.

ज्ञानेन तु तदज्ञानं येषां नाशितमात्मनः ।
तेषामादित्यवज्ज्ञानं प्रकाशयति तत्परम् ॥ 16

But for those whose ignorance of the self has been destroyed
by knowledge, knowledge illumines that Supreme Reality
like the sun.

तद्बुद्धयस्तदात्मानस्तन्निष्ठास्तत्परायणाः ।
गच्छन्त्यपुनरावृत्तिं ज्ञाननिर्धूतकल्मषाः ॥ 17

Having their minds fixed on that, with their selves directed toward that, relying on that and devoted to that, they reach the end of transmigration with their moral stains washed away by knowledge.

विद्याविनयसंपन्ने ब्राह्मणे गवि हस्तिनि ।
शुनि चैव श्वपाके च पण्डिताः समदर्शिनः ॥ 18

Learned men see no difference between a skilled and well-mannered Brahmin, a cow, an elephant, even a dog or an eater of dogs.

इहैव तैर्जितः सर्गो येषां साम्ये स्थितं मनः ।
निर्दोषं हि समं ब्रह्म तस्माद्ब्रह्मणि ते स्थिताः ॥ 19

Even in this world, creation is conquered by those whose mind is based on impartiality. Brahman is flawless and impartial, therefore they are established in Brahman.

न प्रहृष्येत्प्रियं प्राप्य नोद्विजेत्प्राप्य चाप्रियम् ।
स्थिरबुद्धिरसंमूढो ब्रह्मविद्ब्रह्मणि स्थितः ॥ 20

One should not rejoice at obtaining something pleasant, nor grieve when obtaining something unpleasant. The calm and clearheaded knower of Brahman has his foothold in Brahman.

बाह्यस्पर्शेष्वसक्तात्मा विन्दत्यात्मनि यत्सुखम् ।
स ब्रह्मयोगयुक्तात्मा सुखमक्षयमश्नुते ॥ 21

Without attaching his self to external sense impressions, he
finds the happiness that is in himself. This man whose self is
engaged in the discipline of Brahman achieves undying bliss.

ये हि संस्पर्शजा भोगा दुःखयोनय एव ते ।
आद्यन्तवन्तः कौन्तेय न तेषु रमते बुधः ॥ 22

For the experiences that arise from sense impressions are only
sources of sorrow. They have a beginning and an end, Son
of Kunti. The wise take no pleasure in them.

शक्नोतीहैव यः सोढुं प्राक्शरीरविमोक्षणात् ।
कामक्रोधोद्भवं वेगं स युक्तः स सुखी नरः ॥ 23

He who—even in this world, before he is released from his
body—is able to resist the impulse arising from desire and
anger, he is mentally disciplined, he is a happy man.

योऽन्तःसुखोऽन्तरारामस्तथान्तर्ज्योतिरेव यः ।
स योगी ब्रह्मनिर्वाणं ब्रह्मभूतोऽधिगच्छति ॥ 24

He who is happy within, he who is delighted within, and who
finds light within, he is a yogi. Having become Brahman,
he attains the beatitude of Brahman.

लभन्ते ब्रह्मनिर्वाणमृषयः क्षीणकल्मषाः ।
छिन्नद्वैधा यतात्मानः सर्वभूतहिते रताः ॥ 25

Seers whose sins have been worn away acquire the beatitude of Brahman. Having resolved their doubts, with their self under control, they delight in the welfare of all beings.

कामक्रोधवियुक्तानां यतीनां यतचेतसाम् ।
अभितो ब्रह्मनिर्वाणं वर्तते विदितात्मनाम् ॥ 26

The beatitude of Brahman is nigh for ascetics who have disciplined their desire and anger, controlled their minds, and know the self.

स्पर्शान्कृत्वा बहिर्बाह्यांश्चक्षुश्चैवान्तरे भ्रुवोः ।
प्राणापानौ समौ कृत्वा नासाभ्यन्तरचारिणौ ॥ 27
यतेन्द्रियमनोबुद्धिर्मुनिर्मोक्षपरायणः ।
विगतेच्छाभयक्रोधो यः सदा मुक्त एव सः ॥ 28

Shutting out external sense impressions, fixing his vision between the eyebrows, equalizing the inhalation and exhalation moving inside the nostrils: The sage who controls his intellect, mind, and senses; is intent on release; and has cast away desire, fear, and anger—he is forever released.

भोक्तारं यज्ञतपसां सर्वलोकमहेश्वरम् ।
सुहृदं सर्वभूतानां ज्ञात्वा मां शान्तिमृच्छति ॥ 29

When he has acknowledged me as the recipient of sacrifices and austerities, as the great Lord of the whole world, as the friend of all beings, he attains peace.'

इति श्रीमहाभारते शतसाहस्रायां संहितायां श्रीमद्भगवद्गीतायां ब्रह्मविद्या-

शास्त्रे श्रीकृष्णार्जुनसंवादे संन्यासयोगो नाम पञ्चमोऽध्यायः ॥

Thus ends the fifth chapter, entitled "The Reflection upon Renunciation," in the instruction which teaches the sacred knowledge given by the exalted Krishna in his conversation with Arjuna, the auspicious Bhagavad Gita, which is in the work of a hundred thousand verses, the glorious *Mahabharata*.

षष्ठोऽध्यायः

Chapter Six

Meditation

श्रीभगवानुवाच ।
अनाश्रितः कर्मफलं कार्यं कर्म करोति यः ।
स संन्यासी च योगी च न निरग्निर्न चाक्रियः ॥ 1

The Lord said, 'He who performs an action that has to be done without relying on the action's fruit, he is a renouncer and a yogi—not the one without a sacred fire who neglects his rites.

यं संन्यासमिति प्राहुर्योगं तं विद्धि पाण्डव ।
न ह्यसंन्यस्तसंकल्पो योगी भवति कश्चन ॥ 2

Know, Son of Pandu, that what they call renunciation, that is Yoga. For there is no yogi who has not renounced intentionality.

आरुरुक्षोर्मुनेर्योगं कर्म कारणमुच्यते ।
योगारूढस्य तस्यैव शमः कारणमुच्यते ॥ 3

For a sage who wishes to rise to this Yoga, action is said to be the means. When he has risen to this Yoga, serenity is said to be the means.

यदा हि नेन्द्रियार्थेषु न कर्मस्वनुषज्जते ।
सर्वसंकल्पसंन्यासी योगारूढस्तदोच्यते ॥ 4

For only then is he said to have attained Yoga—when he no longer attaches himself to sense objects or actions, and has renounced all intentions.

उद्धरेदात्मनात्मानं नात्मानमवसादयेत् ।
आत्मैव ह्यात्मनो बन्धुरात्मैव रिपुरात्मनः ॥ 5

He should lift his self up by his self; he should not let his self sink down. The self alone is the friend of the self; the self alone is the enemy of the self.

बन्धुरात्मात्मनस्तस्य येनात्मैवात्मना जितः ।
अनात्मनस्तु शत्रुत्वे वर्तेतात्मैव शत्रुवत् ॥ 6

The self is a friend to that self by which self the self has been conquered. But the self of a man with an unconquered self would act in hostility like an enemy.

जितात्मनः प्रशान्तस्य परमात्मा समाहितः ।
शीतोष्णसुखदुःखेषु तथा मानावमानयोः ॥ 7

The higher self of the man who has conquered his self and reached tranquility remains composed in cold, heat, happiness, and sorrow, as well as in honor and dishonor.

ज्ञानविज्ञानतृप्तात्मा कूटस्थो विजितेन्द्रियः ।
युक्त इत्युच्यते योगी समलोष्टाश्मकाञ्चनः ॥ 8

The yogi whose self enjoys knowledge and discrimination, who remains unchangeable after conquering his senses, he is said to be "disciplined." To him, a lump of clay, a stone, and a piece of gold are the same.

सुहृन्मित्रार्युदासीनमध्यस्थद्वेष्यबन्धुषु ।
साधुष्वपि च पापेषु समबुद्धिर्विशिष्यते ॥ 9

He distinguishes himself with the same attitude toward friends, allies, enemies, uninvolved and neutral parties, hateful folks, and relatives—even toward saints and criminals.

योगी युञ्जीत सततमात्मानं रहसि स्थितः ।
एकाकी यतचित्तात्मा निराशीरपरिग्रहः ॥ 10

The yogi should always discipline his self while remaining in solitude, alone, with his mind and self under control, without expectations, without possessions.

शुचौ देशे प्रतिष्ठाप्य स्थिरमासनमात्मनः ।
नात्युच्छ्रितं नातिनीचं चैलाजिनकुशोत्तरम् ॥ 11
तत्रैकाग्रं मनः कृत्वा यतचित्तेन्द्रियक्रियः ।
उपविश्यासने युञ्ज्याद्योगमात्मविशुद्धये ॥ 12

Having firmly established his seat in a pure place—not too high and not too low, with a cover of cloth, deerskin, and kusha grass—he should sit there with his thoughts, senses, and actions under control and practice Yoga, pinpointing his mind for the purification of his self.

समं कायशिरोग्रीवं धारयन्नचलं स्थिरः ।
संप्रेक्ष्य नासिकाग्रं स्वं दिशश्चानवलोकयन् ॥ 13
प्रशान्तात्मा विगतभीर्ब्रह्मचारिव्रते स्थितः ।
मनः संयम्य मच्चित्तो युक्त आसीत मत्परः ॥ 14

Holding his body, head, and neck straight, immobile, and
steady, gazing at the tip of his nose without looking toward
the horizon, with a tranquil mind, fearless, remaining in his
vow of chastity, controlling his mind, and thinking of me, he
should sit disciplined and intent on me.

युञ्जन्नेवं सदात्मानं योगी नियतमानसः ।
शान्तिं निर्वाणपरमां मत्संस्थामधिगच्छति ॥ 15

The yogi who always disciplines his self thusly obtains peace,
the highest beatitude, which rests in me.

नात्यश्नतस्तु योगोऽस्ति न चैकान्तमनश्नतः ।
न चातिस्वप्नशीलस्य जाग्रतो नैव चार्जुन ॥ 16

But Yoga, Arjuna, is neither for the man who eats too much or
who doesn't eat at all, nor for the man who sleeps too much
or who goes without sleep.

युक्ताहारविहारस्य युक्तचेष्टस्य कर्मसु ।
युक्तस्वप्नावबोधस्य योगो भवति दुःखहा ॥ 17

Yoga dispels the sorrows of a man who restrains his diet and
diversions, whose motions are measured when he acts, and
who balances sleep and wakefulness.

यदा विनियतं चित्तमात्मन्येवावतिष्ठते ।
निःस्पृहः सर्वकामेभ्यो युक्त इत्युच्यते तदा ॥ 18

When the restrained mind is established in the self alone, then
the man liberated from all desires is said to be "disciplined."

यथा दीपो निवातस्थो नेङ्गते सोपमा स्मृता ।
योगिनो यतचित्तस्य युञ्जतो योगमात्मनः ॥ 19

"As a lamp sheltered from the wind does not flicker." This
is the well-known simile of the yogi who has controlled his
mind and practices the discipline of the self.

यत्रोपरमते चित्तं निरुद्धं योगसेवया ।
यत्र चैवात्मनात्मानं पश्यन्नात्मनि तुष्यति ॥ 20
सुखमात्यन्तिकं यत्तद्बुद्धिग्राह्यमतीन्द्रियम् ।
वेत्ति यत्र न चैवायं स्थितश्चलति तत्त्वतः ॥ 21
यं लब्ध्वा चापरं लाभं मन्यते नाधिकं ततः ।
यस्मिन्स्थितो न दुःखेन गुरुणापि विचाल्यते ॥ 22
तं विद्याद्दुःखसंयोगवियोगं योगसंज्ञितम् ।
स निश्चयेन योक्तव्यो योगोऽनिर्विण्णचेतसा ॥ 23

When thought settles down, restrained by the practice of
Yoga, and when indeed he rejoices in the self seeing the self
by means of the self; when he knows an infinite bliss which
must be grasped by the mind, a bliss beyond the senses, and
standing on which he remains truly unmovable; when he has
acquired this bliss and he understands there is no other acqui-
sition beyond it, when he rests on it and is not swayed even by
profound sorrow, then he should know that this bliss, called

Yoga, unbinds his union with sorrow. This Yoga should be practiced with determination and a happy heart.

संकल्पप्रभवान्कामांस्त्यक्त्वा सर्वानशेषतः ।
मनसैवेन्द्रियग्रामं विनियम्य समन्ततः ॥ 24
शनैः शनैरुपरमेद्बुद्ध्या धृतिगृहीतया ।
आत्मसंस्थं मनः कृत्वा न किंचिदपि चिन्तयेत् ॥ 25

Leaving behind all desires originating in intention without exception, controlling the multitude of his senses all around, he should little by little settle down, with his mind grasped by resolution. Basing his mind on his self, he should not think of anything at all.

यतो यतो निश्चरति मनश्चञ्चलमस्थिरम् ।
ततस्ततो नियम्यैतदात्मन्येव वशं नयेत् ॥ 26

Whenever the volatile and unsteady mind moves astray, he should restrain it and subdue it in the self.

प्रशान्तमनसं ह्येनं योगिनं सुखमुत्तमम् ।
उपैति शान्तरजसं ब्रह्मभूतमकल्मषम् ॥ 27

For supreme happiness comes to this yogi whose passions are at rest, who, stainless, has become Brahman.

युञ्जन्नेवं सदात्मानं योगी विगतकल्मषः ।
सुखेन ब्रह्मसंस्पर्शमत्यन्तं सुखमश्नुते ॥ 28

Thus, always disciplining his self, the stainless yogi easily
obtains the infinite bliss of contact with Brahman.

सर्वभूतस्थमात्मानं सर्वभूतानि चात्मनि ।
ईक्षते योगयुक्तात्मा सर्वत्र समदर्शनः ॥ 29

The man absorbed in Yoga sees his self in all beings, and all
beings in his self. He sees the same in everything.

यो मां पश्यति सर्वत्र सर्वं च मयि पश्यति ।
तस्याहं न प्रणश्यामि स च मे न प्रणश्यति ॥ 30

I am not lost for him who sees me in all things and sees everything in me, nor is he lost for me.

सर्वभूतस्थितं यो मां भजत्येकत्वमास्थितः ।
सर्वथा वर्तमानोऽपि स योगी मयि वर्तते ॥ 31

He who worships me as existing in all beings, relying on unity,
no matter how he is acting—this yogi is acting in me.

आत्मौपम्येन सर्वत्र समं पश्यति योऽर्जुन ।
सुखं वा यदि वा दुःखं स योगी परमो मतः ॥ 32

He who, comparing other beings with himself, sees the same
in everything, whether it is happiness or sorrow, he, Arjuna, is
known as the perfect yogi.'

अर्जुन उवाच ।
योऽयं योगस्त्वया प्रोक्तः साम्येन मधुसूदन ।

एतस्याहं न पश्यामि चञ्चलत्वात्स्थितिं स्थिराम् ॥ 33

Arjuna said, 'This Yoga that you declared as equanimity, Madhusudana, I cannot see that it has a stable state, given our unsteadiness.

चञ्चलं हि मनः कृष्ण प्रमाथि बलवद्दृढम् ।
तस्याहं निग्रहं मन्ये वायोरिव सुदुष्करम् ॥ 34

For the mind is unsteady, Krishna—troubling, powerful, and resolute. I believe it is as difficult to suppress as the wind.'

श्रीभगवानुवाच ।
असंशयं महाबाहो मनो दुर्निग्रहं चलम् ।
अभ्यासेन तु कौन्तेय वैराग्येण च गृह्यते ॥ 35

The Lord said, 'Undoubtedly, Mighty-armed Prince. The mind is restless and difficult to suppress. But through increasing practice, Son of Kunti, and nonattachment to the world, one can get a grip on it.

असंयतात्मना योगो दुष्प्राप इति मे मतिः ।
वश्यात्मना तु यतता शक्योऽवाप्तुमुपायतः ॥ 36

I agree that Yoga is hard to achieve by a man without self-control. But through proper means it can be achieved by a man exerting himself with his self subdued.'

अर्जुन उवाच ।
अयतिः श्रद्धयोपेतो योगाच्चलितमानसः ।

अप्राप्य योगसंसिद्धिं कां गतिं कृष्ण गच्छति ॥ 37

Arjuna said, 'What fate, Krishna, befalls the man without control, whose mind strays from Yoga although he has faith, when he has failed to achieve perfection in Yoga?

कच्चिन्नोभयविभ्रष्टश्छिन्नाभ्रमिव नश्यति ।
अप्रतिष्ठो महाबाहो विमूढो ब्रह्मणः पथि ॥ 38

Does he not perish like a burst cloud, Mighty-armed Prince, fallen from both, without foundation, and deluded on the path of Brahman?

एतन्मे संशयं कृष्ण छेत्तुमर्हस्यशेषतः ।
त्वदन्यः संशयस्यास्य छेत्ता न ह्युपपद्यते ॥ 39

Please, Krishna, dispel my doubt completely, for there is no one else but you who can dispel this doubt.'

श्रीभगवानुवाच ।
पार्थ नैवेह नामुत्र विनाशस्तस्य विद्यते ।
न हि कल्याणकृत्कश्चिद्दुर्गतिं तात गच्छति ॥ 40

The Lord said, 'Son of Pritha, there is no destruction for him, here in this world or in the next. For, my friend, no misfortune will befall one who does good.

प्राप्य पुण्यकृतॉल्लोकानुषित्वा शाश्वतीः समाः ।
शुचीनां श्रीमतां गेहे योगभ्रष्टोऽभिजायते ॥ 41

Having reached the worlds of those whose acts were virtuous and stayed there very many years, the man fallen from Yoga is reborn in the house of pure and prosperous people.

अथ वा योगिनामेव कुले भवति धीमताम् ।
एतद्धि दुर्लभतरं लोके जन्म यदीदृशम् ॥ ४२

Or, he is born into a family of yogis who are endowed with wisdom. A birth like that is more difficult to obtain in this world.

तत्र तं बुद्धिसंयोगं लभते पौर्वदेहिकम् ।
यतते च ततो भूयः संसिद्धौ कुरुनन्दन ॥ ४३

There he recovers the disposition of his former body, after which he exerts himself even more for its perfection, Joy of the Kurus.

पूर्वाभ्यासेन तेनैव ह्रियते ह्यवशोऽपि सः ।
जिज्ञासुरपि योगस्य शब्दब्रह्मातिवर्तते ॥ ४४

He is sustained precisely by this former practice, even involuntarily, and, eager to learn Yoga, he proceeds beyond the Brahman of the Vedas.

प्रयत्नाद्यतमानस्तु योगी संशुद्धकिल्बिषः ।
अनेकजन्मसंसिद्धस्ततो याति परां गतिम् ॥ ४५

So the yogi, striving assiduously, cleansed of his taints, who has perfected himself through many births, then reaches the highest state.

तपस्विभ्योऽधिको योगी ज्ञानिभ्योऽपि मतोऽधिकः ।
कर्मिभ्यश्चाधिको योगी तस्माद्योगी भवार्जुन ॥ 46

The yogi is deemed to be greater than the ascetics, greater
than the sages, and greater than performers of actions.
Therefore, Arjuna, be a yogi.

योगिनामपि सर्वेषां मद्गतेनान्तरात्मना ।
श्रद्धावान्भजते यो मां स मे युक्ततमो मतः ॥ 47

And of all the yogis, he who faithfully worships me with
his inner self absorbed in me, he is to me the man of
greatest discipline.'

इति श्रीमहाभारते शतसाहस्रायां संहितायां श्रीमद्भगवद्गीतायां
ब्रह्मविद्याशास्त्रे श्रीकृष्णार्जुनसंवादे ध्यानयोगो नाम षष्ठोऽध्यायः ॥

Thus ends the sixth chapter, entitled "The Reflection upon
Meditation," in the instruction which teaches the sacred
knowledge given by the exalted Krishna in his conversation
with Arjuna, the auspicious Bhagavad Gita, which is in the
work of a hundred thousand verses, the glorious *Mahabharata*.

सप्तमोऽध्यायः

Chapter Seven

Knowledge
and Discernment

श्रीभगवानुवाच ।
मय्यासक्तमनाः पार्थ योगं युञ्जन्मदाश्रयः ।
असंशयं समग्रं मां यथा ज्ञास्यसि तच्छृणु ॥ 1

The Lord said, 'With your mind fixed on me, Son of Pritha, practicing Yoga with me as your refuge, hear this, so that you will know me completely and without a doubt.

ज्ञानं तेऽहं सविज्ञानमिदं वक्ष्याम्यशेषतः ।
यज्ज्ञात्वा नेह भूयोऽन्यज्ज्ञातव्यमवशिष्यते ॥ 2

I will teach you this knowledge, together with the faculty of discrimination, in its entirety. When you have learned this, nothing else in this world remains to be known.

मनुष्याणां सहस्रेषु कश्चिद्यतति सिद्धये ।
यततामपि सिद्धानां कश्चिन्मां वेत्ति तत्त्वतः ॥ 3

Among thousands of people, perhaps one strives for success, and of the successful ones, perhaps one knows me truly.

भूमिरापोऽनलो वायुः खं मनो बुद्धिरेव च ।
अहंकार इतीयं मे भिन्ना प्रकृतिरष्टधा ॥ ४

My primordial nature is divided into these eight factors: earth, water, fire, wind, ether, mind, intellect, and ego-consciousness.

अपरेयमितस्त्वन्यां प्रकृतिं विद्धि मे पराम् ।
जीवभूतां महाबाहो ययेदं धार्यते जगत् ॥ ५

This is my lower nature, but know my other and higher nature, the substance of life, Mighty-armed Prince! By this the world is sustained.

एतद्योनीनि भूतानि सर्वाणीत्युपधारय ।
अहं कृत्स्नस्य जगतः प्रभवः प्रलयस्तथा ॥ ६

Know that all beings have this as their source. I am the origin and the dissolution of this whole world.

मत्तः परतरं नान्यत्किंचिदस्ति धनंजय ।
मयि सर्वमिदं प्रोतं सूत्रे मणिगणा इव ॥ ७

There is nothing higher than me, Dhananjaya! This entire world is strung on me like pearls on a string.

रसोऽहमप्सु कौन्तेय प्रभास्मि शशिसूर्ययोः ।
प्रणवः सर्ववेदेषु शब्दः खे पौरुषं नृषु ॥ ८

Son of Kunti, I am the taste in the waters, I am the splendor in the moon and the sun, the syllable *om* in all the Vedas, the sound in ether, manliness in men.

पुण्यो गन्धः पृथिव्यां च तेजश्चास्मि विभावसौ ।
जीवनं सर्वभूतेषु तपश्चास्मि तपस्विषु ॥ 9

I am also the pure fragrance in the earth and the brightness in fire. I am the life in all beings and the austerity in all ascetics.

बीजं मां सर्वभूतानां विद्धि पार्थ सनातनम् ।
बुद्धिर्बुद्धिमतामस्मि तेजस्तेजस्विनामहम् ॥ 10

Know, Son of Pritha, that I am the eternal seed of all beings. I am the intellect of the intelligent, the splendor of the splendid.

बलं बलवतां चाहं कामरागविवर्जितम् ।
धर्माविरुद्धो भूतेषु कामोऽस्मि भरतर्षभ ॥ 11

I am the strength in the strong, but without desire and passion. I am the desire in beings, Bull of the Bharatas, but desire consistent with the law.

ये चैव सात्त्विका भावा राजसास्तामसाश्च ये ।
मत्त एवेति तान्विद्धि न त्वहं तेषु ते मयि ॥ 12

And the states of being marked by clarity, as also the ones marked by agitation and sluggishness. Know that these come from me, but I am not in them. They are in me.

त्रिभिर्गुणमयैर्भावैरेभिः सर्वमिदं जगत् ।
मोहितं नाभिजानाति मामेभ्यः परमव्ययम् ॥ 13

The whole world is deluded by these three states of being produced by the properties. It does not know that I am above them, imperishable.

दैवी होषा गुणमयी मम माया दुरत्यया ।
मामेव ये प्रपद्यन्ते मायामेतां तरन्ति ते ॥ 14

For this divine illusory power of mine, produced by the properties, is hard to escape. Only those who take refuge in me overcome this power of illusion.

न मां दुष्कृतिनो मूढाः प्रपद्यन्ते नराधमाः ।
माययापहृतज्ञाना आसुरं भावमाश्रिताः ॥ 15

Deluded evildoers, the lowest of men, do not resort to me. Their insight carried away by illusion, they rest in a demonic state of being.

चतुर्विधा भजन्ते मां जनाः सुकृतिनोऽर्जुन ।
आर्तो जिज्ञासुरर्थार्थी ज्ञानी च भरतर्षभ ॥ 16

Wise men of four kinds, Bull of the Bharatas, worship me: the man in distress, the seeker of knowledge, the seeker of wealth, and the man of knowledge.

तेषां ज्ञानी नित्ययुक्त एकभक्तिर्विशिष्यते ।
प्रियो हि ज्ञानिनोऽत्यर्थमहं स च मम प्रियः ॥ 17

Of these, the man of knowledge stands out, always disciplined and with singular devotion. For to the man of knowledge, I am immensely dear, and he is dear to me.

उदाराः सर्व एवैते ज्ञानी त्वात्मैव मे मतम् ।
आस्थितः स हि युक्तात्मा मामेवानुत्तमां गतिम् ॥ 18

All these are noble indeed, but I think that the man of knowledge is the self itself. For, with a disciplined self, he relies on me alone as the ultimate destination.

बहूनां जन्मनामन्ते ज्ञानवान्मां प्रपद्यते ।
वासुदेवः सर्वमिति स महात्मा सुदुर्लभः ॥ 19

At the end of many births, the man of knowledge reaches me, thinking "Vasudeva is everything." Such a great-souled man is hard to find.

कामैस्तैस्तैर्हृतज्ञानाः प्रपद्यन्तेऽन्यदेवताः ।
तं तं नियममास्थाय प्रकृत्या नियताः स्वया ॥ 20

Those whose knowledge has been ravished by so many desires resort to other deities, relying on this or that observance, constrained by their own nature.

यो यो यां यां तनुं भक्तः श्रद्धयार्चितुमिच्छति ।
तस्य तस्याचलां श्रद्धां तामेव विदधाम्यहम् ॥ 21

Whichever form a devoted man wishes to praise with faith, I make that very faith unshakeable in him, whoever he is.

स तया श्रद्धया युक्तस्तस्या राधनमीहते ।
लभते च ततः कामान्मयैव विहितान्हि तान् ॥ 22

Endowed with this faith, he aspires to propitiate that form,
and through it his desires are fulfilled, for they are provided
by no one but me.

अन्तवत्तु फलं तेषां तद्भवत्यल्पमेधसाम् ।
देवान्देवयजो यान्ति मद्भक्ता यान्ति मामपि ॥ 23

But it is an ephemeral fruit that these men of little insight
obtain. Those who sacrifice to the gods, go to the gods. But
those who are devoted to me, come to me.

अव्यक्तं व्यक्तिमापन्नं मन्यन्ते मामबुद्धयः ।
परं भावमजानन्तो ममाव्ययमनुत्तमम् ॥ 24

The unintelligent think of me as an unmanifest being having
become manifest, not knowing my highest state of being,
which is imperishable and incomparable.

नाहं प्रकाशः सर्वस्य योगमायासमावृतः ।
मूढोऽयं नाभिजानाति लोको मामजमव्ययम् ॥ 25

Clouded by the illusion of my magic power, I am not visible
to all. This deluded world does not recognize me as unborn
and imperishable.

वेदाहं समतीतानि वर्तमानानि चार्जुन ।
भविष्याणि च भूतानि मां तु वेद न कश्चन ॥ 26

I know the beings of the past, of the present, and of the future, Arjuna, but no one knows me.

इच्छाद्वेषसमुत्थेन द्वंद्वमोहेन भारत ।
सर्वभूतानि संमोहं सर्गे यान्ति परंतप ॥ 27

At creation, Scorcher of Enemies, all beings become utterly stupefied by the delusion of opposites arising from attraction and repulsion.

येषां त्वन्तगतं पापं जनानां पुण्यकर्मणाम् ।
ते द्वंद्वमोहनिर्मुक्ता भजन्ते मां दृढव्रताः ॥ 28

But the men of meritorious deeds, whose evil has come to an end, are released from the delusion of opposites and worship me, firm in their vows.

जरामरणमोक्षाय मामाश्रित्य यतन्ति ये ।
ते ब्रह्म तद्विदुः कृत्स्नमध्यात्मं कर्म चाखिलम् ॥ 29

Those who strive for release from old age and death by relying on me, they know that this is Brahman, everything that pertains to the self, and action unabridged.

साधिभूताधिदैवं मां साधियज्ञं च ये विदुः ।
प्रयाणकालेऽपि च मां ते विदुर्युक्तचेतसः ॥ 30

Those who know me as the material substratum, as the supreme deity, and as the principal sacrifice, they know me, their minds disciplined, even when they depart from this world.'

इति श्रीमहाभारते शतसाहस्रायां संहितायां श्रीमद्भगवद्गीतायां ब्रह्मविद्या-
शास्त्रे श्रीकृष्णार्जुनसंवादे ज्ञानविज्ञानयोगारव्यः सप्तमोऽध्यायः ॥

Thus ends the seventh chapter, entitled "The Reflection upon Knowledge and Discernment," in the instruction which teaches the sacred knowledge given by the exalted Krishna in his conversation with Arjuna, the auspicious Bhagavad Gita, which is in the work of a hundred thousand verses, the glorious *Mahabharata*.

Chapter Eight

The Liberating Brahman

अर्जुन उवाच ।
किं तद्ब्रह्म किमध्यात्मं किं कर्म पुरुषोत्तम ।
अधिभूतं च किं प्रोक्तमधिदैवं किमुच्यते ॥ 1

Arjuna said, 'What is this Brahman, this individual self, and
this action, you best of men? What is said to be the material
substratum and what the divine agent?

अधियज्ञः कथं कोऽत्र देहेऽस्मिन्मधुसूदन ।
प्रयाणकाले च कथं ज्ञेयोऽसि नियतात्मभिः ॥ 2

What is the principal sacrifice, Madhusudana, and how is it
here in this body? And how can the self-controlled know you
at the time of departure from this world?'

श्रीभगवानुवाच ।
अक्षरं ब्रह्म परमं स्वभावोऽध्यात्ममुच्यते ।
भूतभावोद्भवकरो विसर्गः कर्मसंज्ञितः ॥ 3

The Lord said, 'The immutable Brahman is called the
supreme, the Brahmic part of one's nature is called the

individual self, and the creating which brings beings into existence is called action.

अधिभूतं क्षरो भावः पुरुषश्चाधिदैवतम् ।
अधियज्ञोऽहमेवात्र देहे देहभृतां वर ॥ ४

The material substratum is transitory existence and the spirit is the supreme deity. I, indeed, am the principal sacrifice in this body, you best of embodied souls.

अन्तकाले च मामेव स्मरन्मुक्त्वा कलेवरम् ।
यः प्रयाति स मद्भावं याति नास्त्यत्र संशयः ॥ ५

And at the time of death, the man who leaves his body thinking of me alone reaches my state of being. There is no doubt about it.

यं यं वापि स्मरन्भावं त्यजत्यन्ते कलेवरम् ।
तं तमेवैति कौन्तेय सदा तद्भावभावितः ॥ ६

Whatever is on his mind when he leaves his body in his final hour, that he will reach, Son of Kunti. His condition is always determined by that.

तस्मात्सर्वेषु कालेषु मामनुस्मर युध्य च ।
मय्यर्पितमनोबुद्धिर्मामेवैष्यस्यसंशयः ॥ ७

Therefore, remember me at all times and fight! With your mind and intellect fixed on me, you will undoubtedly come to me alone.

अभ्यासयोगयुक्तेन चेतसा नान्यगामिना ।
परमं पुरुषं दिव्यं याति पार्थानुचिन्तयन् ॥ 8

He who meditates with a mind trained by the discipline of
repeated practice, not straying elsewhere, reaches the supreme,
divine spirit, Son of Pritha.

कविं पुराणमनुशासितारमणोरणीयांसमनुस्मरेद्यः ।
सर्वस्य धातारमचिन्त्यरूपमादित्यवर्णं तमसः परस्तात् ॥ 9
प्रयाणकाले मनसाचलेन भक्त्या युक्तो योगबलेन चैव ।
भ्रुवोर्मध्ये प्राणमावेश्य सम्यक्स तं परं पुरुषमुपैति दिव्यम् ॥ 10

He who, at the time of departure from this world, would
remember the ancient sage, the preceptor, smaller than an
atom, the creator of all, of inconceivable form, and having
a sunny color beyond darkness; he who is endowed with an
unshaken mind, devotion, the power of mental discipline, and
concentrates his breath between his eyebrows, he reaches this
supreme, divine spirit.

यदक्षरं वेदविदो वदन्ति विशन्ति यद्यतयो वीतरागाः ।
यदिच्छन्तो ब्रह्मचर्यं चरन्ति तत्ते पदं संग्रहेण प्रवक्ष्ये ॥ 11

I will briefly explain to you the abode that the knowers of the
Vedas call immutable. The ascetics of subdued passions want
to enter it and live a chaste life of study.

सर्वद्वाराणि संयम्य मनो हृदि निरुध्य च ।
मूर्ध्न्याधायात्मनः प्राणमास्थितो योगधारणाम् ॥ 12
ओमित्येकाक्षरं ब्रह्म व्याहरन्मामनुस्मरन् ।

यः प्रयाति त्यजन्देहं स याति परमां गतिम् ॥ 13

Closing all the gates of the body, confining his mind within
his heart, holding within his head the breath of the self,
and relying on the concentration produced by Yoga, he
who departs, leaving his body while uttering the Brahman
expressed in the single syllable *om* and remembering me, he
reaches the supreme state.

अनन्यचेताः सततं यो मां स्मरति नित्यशः ।
तस्याहं सुलभः पार्थ नित्ययुक्तस्य योगिनः ॥ 14

He who always thinks of me without his mind ever straying to
another, that yogi, under permanent control, finds me easy to
reach, Son of Pritha.

मामुपेत्य पुनर्जन्म दुःखालयमशाश्वतम् ।
नाप्नुवन्ति महात्मानः संसिद्धिं परमां गताः ॥ 15

The great souls who come to me do not return to rebirth,
that ephemeral realm of sorrow. They have reached
supreme perfection.

आ ब्रह्मभुवनाल्लोकाः पुनरावर्तिनोऽर्जुन ।
मामुपेत्य तु कौन्तेय पुनर्जन्म न विद्यते ॥ 16

All the way to the realm of Brahma, the worlds repeatedly
return, Arjuna. But if you come to me, Son of Kunti, there is
no rebirth anymore.

सहस्रयुगपर्यन्तमहर्यद्ब्रह्मणो विदुः ।
रात्रिं युगसहस्रान्तां तेऽहोरात्रविदो जनाः ॥ 17

Those expert in days and nights know that a day of Brahma
encompasses a thousand eons, and a night of Brahma ends
after a thousand eons.

अव्यक्ताद्व्यक्तयः सर्वाः प्रभवन्त्यहरागमे ।
रात्र्यागमे प्रलीयन्ते तत्रैवाव्यक्तसंज्ञके ॥ 18

All manifestations arise from the unmanifest at the break of
day. As night falls, they are dissolved in this very thing called
the unmanifest.

भूतग्रामः स एवायं भूत्वा भूत्वा प्रलीयते ।
रात्र्यागमेऽवशः पार्थ प्रभवत्यहरागमे ॥ 19

This multitude of beings comes into existence again and again
and dissolves helplessly at the fall of night, Son of Pritha. At
daybreak, it is born again.

परस्तस्मात्तु भावोऽन्योऽव्यक्तोऽव्यक्तात्सनातनः ।
यः स सर्वेषु भूतेषु नश्यत्सु न विनश्यति ॥ 20

But there is a higher being beyond this, unmanifest beyond
the unmanifest, eternal, who does not perish when all
beings perish.

अव्यक्तोऽक्षर इत्युक्तस्तमाहुः परमां गतिम् ।
यं प्राप्य न निवर्तन्ते तद्धाम परमं मम ॥ 21

This unmanifest is called the imperishable. This is what they call the ultimate state. When they have reached this, they don't return. This is my supreme abode.

पुरुषः स परः पार्थ भक्त्या लभ्यस्त्वनन्यया ।
यस्यान्तःस्थानि भूतानि येन सर्वमिदं ततम् ॥ 22

This is the supreme spirit, Son of Pritha, attainable only through undeviating devotion, in whom beings abide, on whom all this is strung.

यत्र काले त्वनावृत्तिमावृत्तिं चैव योगिनः ।
प्रयाता यान्ति तं कालं वक्ष्यामि भरतर्षभ ॥ 23

Now, Bull of the Bharatas, I shall explain at which time the yogis who have departed life return or do not return.

अग्निर्ज्योतिरहः शुक्लः षण्मासा उत्तरायणम् ।
तत्र प्रयाता गच्छन्ति ब्रह्म ब्रह्मविदो जनाः ॥ 24

The scholars of Brahman who depart life by fire, by sunlight, by day, in the bright fortnight, and during the six months after the winter solstice called the northern path, go to Brahman.

धूमो रात्रिस्तथा कृष्णः षण्मासा दक्षिणायनम् ।
तत्र चान्द्रमसं ज्योतिर्योगी प्राप्य निवर्तते ॥ 25

The yogi who reaches the light of the moon by smoke, by night, in the dark fortnight, and during the six months after the summer solstice called the southern path, returns.

शुक्लकृष्णे गती ह्येते जगतः शाश्वते मते ।
एकया यात्यनावृत्तिमन्ययावर्तते पुनः ॥ 26

These two routes of the world, the light and the dark, are considered to be eternal. By the former, one does not return; by the latter, one returns.

नैते सृती पार्थ जानन्योगी मुह्यति कश्चन ।
तस्मात्सर्वेषु कालेषु योगयुक्तो भवार्जुन ॥ 27

Son of Pritha, no yogi who knows these two routes is deluded. Therefore, Arjuna, you must at all times remain firm in your mental discipline.

वेदेषु यज्ञेषु तपःसु चैव दानेषु यत्पुण्यफलं प्रदिष्टम् ।
अत्येति तत्सर्वमिदं विदित्वा योगी परं स्थानमुपैति चाद्यम् ॥ 28

The yogi transcends it all—the fruits of merit assigned to the Vedas, to sacrifices, to austerities, and to gift giving—when he has understood this and attains the supreme, primordial place.'

इति श्रीमहाभारते शतसाहस्रायां संहितायां श्रीमद्भगवद्गीतायां ब्रह्मविद्या-
शास्त्रे श्रीकृष्णार्जुनसंवादे तारकब्रह्मयोगो नामाष्टमोऽध्यायः ॥

Thus ends the eighth chapter, entitled "The Reflection upon the Liberating Brahman," in the instruction which teaches the sacred knowledge given by the exalted Krishna in his conversation with Arjuna, the auspicious Bhagavad Gita, which is in the work of a hundred thousand verses, the glorious *Mahabharata*.

Chapter Nine

The Royal Science

श्रीभगवानुवाच ।
इदं तु ते गुह्यतमं प्रवक्ष्याम्यनसूयवे ।
ज्ञानं विज्ञानसहितं यज्ज्ञात्वा मोक्ष्यसेऽशुभात् ॥ 1

The Lord said, 'Since you show no spite, I will tell you this profound secret knowledge joined with discrimination. Through this knowledge, you will soon be released.

राजविद्या राजगुह्यं पवित्रमिदमुत्तमम् ।
प्रत्यक्षावगमं धर्म्यं सुसुखं कर्तुमव्ययम् ॥ 2

This is the royal science, the royal secret, the ultimate purification, learned through direct perception, in accordance with the law, very easy to accomplish, and imperishable.

अश्रद्दधानाः पुरुषा धर्मस्यास्य परंतप ।
अप्राप्य मां निवर्तन्ते मृत्युसंसारवर्त्मनि ॥ 3

Men who have no faith in this law, Scorcher of Enemies, do not reach me and return to the path of the circuit of death.

मया ततमिदं सर्वं जगदव्यक्तमूर्तिना ।
मत्स्थानि सर्वभूतानि न चाहं तेष्ववस्थितः ॥ ४

This whole world is pervaded by me in my unmanifest form.
All beings exist in me, but I do not exist in them.

न च मत्स्थानि भूतानि पश्य मे योगमैश्वरम् ।
भूतभृन्न च भूतस्थो ममात्मा भूतभावनः ॥ ५

And yet, the beings do not exist in me—behold my divine
magic power! My self is the source of beings. It sustains them,
but does not exist in them.

यथाकाशस्थितो नित्यं वायुः सर्वत्रगो महान् ।
तथा सर्वाणि भूतानि मत्स्थानीत्युपधारय ॥ ६

Understand that all beings exist in me, like the huge wind
eternally blowing everywhere, yet contained within space.

सर्वभूतानि कौन्तेय प्रकृतिं यान्ति मामिकाम् ।
कल्पक्षये पुनस्तानि कल्पादौ विसृजाम्यहम् ॥ ७

All beings, Son of Kunti, return to my primordial nature at
the end of an eon. At the beginning of the next eon, I produce
them again.

प्रकृतिं स्वामवष्टभ्य विसृजामि पुनः पुनः ।
भूतग्राममिमं कृत्स्नमवशं प्रकृतेर्वशात् ॥ ८

Resorting to the force of my own primordial nature—and through no will of their own—I produce this whole multitude of beings again and again.

न च मां तानि कर्माणि निबध्नन्ति धनंजय ।
उदासीनवदासीनमसक्तं तेषु कर्मसु ॥ ९

Yet these actions do not bind me, Dhananjaya. I sit like an uninvolved king, detached from these actions.

मयाध्यक्षेण प्रकृतिः सूयते सचराचरम् ।
हेतुनानेन कौन्तेय जगद्विपरिवर्तते ॥ १०

Primordial nature is produced with the moving and the unmoving, with my supervision. For that reason, Son of Kunti, the world revolves.

अवजानन्ति मां मूढा मानुषीं तनुमाश्रितम् ।
परं भावमजानन्तो मम भूतमहेश्वरम् ॥ ११

The deluded despise me when I dwell in a human body, not knowing my higher nature as the great lord of beings.

मोघाशा मोघकर्माणो मोघज्ञाना विचेतसः ।
राक्षसीमासुरीं चैव प्रकृतिं मोहिनीं श्रिताः ॥ १२

Mindless, with vain hopes, vain actions, and vain knowledge, they devolve to the deceptive nature of monsters and demons.

महात्मानस्तु मां पार्थ दैवीं प्रकृतिमाश्रिताः ।

भजन्त्यनन्यमनसो ज्ञात्वा भूतादिमव्ययम् ॥ 13

But great-souled men, Son of Pritha, seek refuge in me, the
divine nature. They worship me without thought for anybody
else, knowing me as the imperishable origin of beings.

सततं कीर्तयन्तो मां यतन्तश्च दृढव्रताः ।
नमस्यन्तश्च मां भक्त्या नित्ययुक्ता उपासते ॥ 14

Constantly praising me, striving to keep their vows, and
revering me, they worship me devoutly, always disciplined.

ज्ञानयज्ञेन चाप्यन्ये यजन्तो मामुपासते ।
एकत्वेन पृथक्त्वेन बहुधा विश्वतोमुखम् ॥ 15

Others again sacrifice to me with the sacrifice of knowledge,
and worship me as the one, the multiple, and the manifold,
facing in all directions.

अहं ऋतुरहं यज्ञः स्वधाहमहमौषधम् ।
मन्त्रोऽहमहमेवाज्यमहमग्निरहं हुतम् ॥ 16

I am the rite, I am the sacrifice, I am the libation, I am the
herb, I am the sacrificial formula. It is I who am the butter,
I who am the fire, I who am the offering.

पिताहमस्य जगतो माता धाता पितामहः ।
वेद्यं पवित्रमोंकार ऋक्साम यजुरेव च ॥ 17

I am the father of this world, its mother, supporter, and
grandfather, its object of knowledge, its purifier, the syllable

om, the collection of sacred verses, the collection of chanted hymns, and, indeed, the collection of sacrificial formulas.

गतिर्भर्ता प्रभुः साक्षी निवासः शरणं सुहृत् ।
प्रभवः प्रलयः स्थानं निधानं बीजमव्ययम् ॥ 18

I am the goal, the master, the lord, the witness, the abode, the refuge, and the friend. I am the origin and the dissolution, the foundation, the resting place, and the imperishable seed.

तपाम्यहमहं वर्षं निगृह्णाम्युत्सृजामि च ।
अमृतं चैव मृत्युश्च सदसच्चाहमर्जुन ॥ 19

I give heat, I withhold rain, and I let it pour. I am immortality and death, the existent and the nonexistent, Arjuna.

त्रैविद्या मां सोमपाः पूतपापा यज्ञैरिष्ट्वा स्वर्गतिं प्रार्थयन्ते ।
ते पुण्यमासाद्य सुरेन्द्रलोकमश्नन्ति दिव्यान्दिवि देवभोगान् ॥ 20

Those who know the three Vedas, the soma drinkers whose sins have been cleansed, seek the way to heaven by making sacrifices to me. They reach the pure world of Indra and enjoy the divine pleasures of the gods in heaven.

ते तं भुक्त्वा स्वर्गलोकं विशालं क्षीणे पुण्ये मर्त्यलोकं विशन्ति ।
एवं त्रयीधर्ममनुप्रपन्ना गतागतं कामकामा लभन्ते ॥ 21

When they have enjoyed the wide world of heaven and their merit is exhausted, they return to the world of mortals. Thus, acting in conformance with the laws of the three Vedas and dictated by their passions, they obtain the ephemeral.

अनन्याश्चिन्तयन्तो मां ये जनाः पर्युपासते ।
तेषां नित्याभियुक्तानां योगक्षेमं वहाम्यहम् ॥ 22

To the people who worship me with no one else in mind, forever diligent, I bring welfare and security.

येऽप्यन्यदेवता भक्ता यजन्ते श्रद्धयान्विताः ।
तेऽपि मामेव कौन्तेय यजन्त्यविधिपूर्वकम् ॥ 23

But those devotees of other gods who sacrifice with faith, even they sacrifice to me alone, Son of Kunti, although without the proper rites.

अहं हि सर्वयज्ञानां भोक्ता च प्रभुरेव च ।
न तु मामभिजानन्ति तत्त्वेनातश्च्यवन्ति ते ॥ 24

For I am the enjoyer, and indeed, the lord of all sacrifices. But they do not know me properly and therefore stumble.

यान्ति देवव्रता देवान्पितृन्यान्ति पितृव्रताः ।
भूतानि यान्ति भूतेज्या यान्ति मद्याजिनोऽपि माम् ॥ 25

Those avowed to the gods, go to the gods; those avowed to the fathers, go to the fathers; those who sacrifice to the ghouls, go to the ghouls; but those who sacrifice to me, come to me.

पत्रं पुष्पं फलं तोयं यो मे भक्त्या प्रयच्छति ।

तदहं भक्त्युपहृतमश्नामि प्रयतात्मनः ॥ 26

Whoever, with a disciplined self, devotedly offers me a leaf, a flower, a fruit, or water, I accept that offering of devotion from him.

यत्करोषि यदश्नासि यज्जुहोषि ददासि यत् ।
यत्तपस्यसि कौन्तेय तत्कुरुष्व मदर्पणम् ॥ 27

Whatever you do, whatever you eat, whatever you offer or give, whatever austerities you perform, Son of Kunti, make that an offering to me.

शुभाशुभफलैरेवं मोक्ष्यसे कर्मबन्धनैः ।
संन्यासयोगयुक्तात्मा विमुक्तो मामुपैष्यसि ॥ 28

Thus you will be released from the fetters of karma, whether their fruits are good or bad. With your self controlled by the discipline of renunciation, you will come to me, released.

समोऽहं सर्वभूतेषु न मे द्वेष्योऽस्ति न प्रियः ।
ये भजन्ति तु मां भक्त्या मयि ते तेषु चाप्यहम् ॥ 29

I am impartial to all beings. I neither detest nor prefer any of them. But they who worship me devotedly, they are in me and I am in them.

अपि चेत्सुदुराचारो भजते मामनन्यभाक् ।
साधुरेव स मन्तव्यः सम्यग्व्यवसितो हि सः ॥ 30

If even a man of wicked conduct worships me with singular devotion, he should be regarded as good, for he has the right conviction.

क्षिप्रं भवति धर्मात्मा शश्वच्छान्तिं निगच्छति ।
कौन्तेय प्रतिजानीहि न मे भक्तः प्रणश्यति ॥ 31

His self becomes righteous quickly and he finds lasting peace. Be aware of this, Son of Kunti: No devotee of mine is lost.

मां हि पार्थ व्यपाश्रित्य येऽपि स्युः पापयोनयः ।
स्त्रियो वैश्यास्तथा शूद्रास्तेऽपि यान्ति परां गतिम् ॥ 32

For even those of lowly origin, Son of Pritha, such as women, traders, peasants, and servants, reach the highest state when they take refuge in me.

किं पुनर्ब्राह्मणाः पुण्या भक्ता राजर्षयस्तथा ।
अनित्यमसुखं लोकमिमं प्राप्य भजस्व माम् ॥ 33

How much more pure Brahmin devotees and royal sages? When you live in this transient, unhappy world, worship me!

मन्मना भव मद्भक्तो मद्याजी मां नमस्कुरु ।
मामेवैष्यसि युक्त्वैवमात्मानं मत्परायणः ॥ 34

Direct your thoughts toward me, be devoted to me, sacrifice to me, pay homage to me. By disciplining your self in this way, with me as your final goal, you will reach me.'

इति श्रीमहाभारते शतसाहस्रायां संहितायां श्रीमद्भगवद्गीतायां ब्रह्मविद्याशास्त्रे श्रीकृष्णार्जुनसंवादे राजविद्याराजगुह्ययोगो नाम नवमोऽध्यायः ॥

Thus ends the ninth chapter, entitled "The Reflection upon the Royal Science and the Royal Secrets," in the instruction which teaches the sacred knowledge given by the exalted Krishna in his conversation with Arjuna, the auspicious Bhagavad Gita, which is in the work of a hundred thousand verses, the glorious *Mahabharata*.

दशमोऽध्यायः

Chapter Ten

Power

श्रीभगवानुवाच ।
भूय एव महाबाहो शृणु मे परमं वचः ।
यत्तेऽहं प्रीयमाणाय वक्ष्यामि हितकाम्यया ॥ १

The Lord said, 'Listen once more, Mighty-armed Prince, to
my supreme word. I will pronounce to you who loves me,
for your benefit.

न मे विदुः सुरगणाः प्रभवं न महर्षयः ।
अहमादिर्हि देवानां महर्षीणां च सर्वशः ॥ २

The hosts of gods do not know my origin, nor do the great
sages. For I am, in every way, the source of the gods and
the great sages.

यो मामजमनादिं च वेत्ति लोकमहेश्वरम् ।
असंमूढः स मर्त्येषु सर्वपापैः प्रमुच्यते ॥ ३

He who knows me as unborn, without origin, and as the great
lord of the world, he, clearheaded among mortals, is released
from all sins.

बुद्धिर्ज्ञानमसंमोहः क्षमा सत्यं दमः शमः ।
सुखं दुःखं भवोऽभावो भयं चाभयमेव च ॥ ४
अहिंसा समता तुष्टिस्तपो दानं यशोऽयशः ।
भवन्ति भावा भूतानां मत्त एव पृथग्विधाः ॥ ५

Intellect, knowledge, lack of delusion, patience, veracity, self-control, tranquility, happiness, unhappiness, becoming and annihilation, nonviolence, equableness, contentment, austerity, liberality, fame, and disgrace are the existential modes of beings, springing in their various ways from me alone.

महर्षयः सप्त पूर्वे चत्वारो मनवस्तथा ।
मद्भावा मानसा जाता येषां लोक इमाः प्रजाः ॥ ६

The seven great sages of old and the four Manus were born from my mind, sharing my nature. This world's beings are their descendants.

एतां विभूतिं योगं च मम यो वेत्ति तत्त्वतः ।
सोऽविकम्पेन योगेन युज्यते नात्र संशयः ॥ ७

He who knows this great power and discipline of mine, he is endowed with unfaltering discipline, there is no doubt about it.

अहं सर्वस्य प्रभवो मत्तः सर्वं प्रवर्तते ।
इति मत्वा भजन्ते मां बुधा भावसमन्विताः ॥ ८

I am the origin of all; from me everything comes forth. Knowing thus, the wise worship me filled with affection.

मच्चित्ता मद्गतप्राणा बोधयन्तः परस्परम् ।
कथयन्तश्च मां नित्यं तुष्यन्ति च रमन्ति च ॥ ९

With their thoughts on me, their sense organs absorbed in
me, teaching each other and talking about me, they are always
happy and delighted.

तेषां सततयुक्तानां भजतां प्रीतिपूर्वकम् ।
ददामि बुद्धियोगं तं येन मामुपयान्ति ते ॥ १०

To these joyful worshipers, always disciplined, I give this
discipline of the intellect by which they reach me.

तेषामेवानुकम्पार्थमहमज्ञानजं तमः ।
नाशयाम्यात्मभावस्थो ज्ञानदीपेन भास्वता ॥ ११

It is out of compassion for them that I, relying on my own
nature, destroy the darkness born of ignorance with the
shining light of knowledge.'

अर्जुन उवाच ।
परं ब्रह्म परं धाम पवित्रं परमं भवान् ।
पुरुषं शाश्वतं दिव्यमादिदेवमजं विभुम् ॥ १२
आहुस्त्वामृषयः सर्वे देवर्षिर्नारदस्तथा ।
असितो देवलो व्यासः स्वयं चैव ब्रवीषि मे ॥ १३

Arjuna said, 'All the sages call you the supreme Brahman, the
supreme abode, the supreme purifier, the Lord, the eternal
and divine spirit, the first god, unborn and ubiquitous, and so

do Narada the divine sage, Asita Devala, and Vyasa. Indeed, so you tell me yourself.

सर्वमेतदृतं मन्ये यन्मां वदसि केशव ।
न हि ते भगवन्व्यक्तिं विदुर्देवा न दानवाः ॥ 14

I believe that everything you say is true, Keshava! For neither the gods nor the demons know your manifestation, my Lord.

स्वयमेवात्मनात्मानं वेत्थ त्वं पुरुषोत्तम ।
भूतभावन भूतेश देवदेव जगत्पते ॥ 15

You yourself know your self by your self—you, the supreme spirit, the source of beings, lord of beings, god of gods, master of the world!

वक्तुमर्हस्यशेषेण दिव्या ह्यात्मविभूतयः ।
याभिर्विभूतिभिर्लोकानिमांस्त्वं व्याप्य तिष्ठसि ॥ 16

Please tell me about it all, for the manifestations of your self are wonderful. By means of these manifestations, you keep pervading these worlds.

कथं विद्यामहं योगिंस्त्वां सदा परिचिन्तयन् ।
केषु केषु च भावेषु चिन्त्योऽसि भगवन्मया ॥ 17

How may I, always meditating on you, know you, conjurer? On which aspects of your nature should I meditate, my Lord?

विस्तरेणात्मनो योगं विभूतिं च जनार्दन ।

भूयः कथय तृप्तिर्हि शृण्वतो नास्ति मेऽमृतम् ॥ 18

Tell me again in detail about your Yoga and your manifestation, Janardana! For I have not had enough of listening to
your words of nectar.'

श्रीभगवानुवाच ।
हन्त ते कथयिष्यामि दिव्या ह्यात्मविभूतयः ।
प्राधान्यतः कुरुश्रेष्ठ नास्त्यन्तो विस्तरस्य मे ॥ 19

The Lord said, 'Oh yes, I will tell you about the wonderful
manifestations of my self, but about the most important ones,
Best of the Kurus, for there is no end to my abundance.

अहमात्मा गुडाकेश सर्वभूताशयस्थितः ।
अहमादिश्च मध्यं च भूतानामन्त एव च ॥ 20

I am the self dwelling in the heart of all beings, Gudakesha. I
am the beginning, the middle, and indeed the end of beings.

आदित्यानामहं विष्णुर्ज्योतिषां रविरंशुमान् ।
मरीचिर्मरुतामस्मि नक्षत्राणामहं शशी ॥ 21

Of the Adityas, I am Vishnu; of the celestial lights, I am the
radiant sun. I am Marici among the Maruts; amidst the
constellations, I am the moon.

वेदानां सामवेदोऽस्मि देवानामस्मि वासवः ।
इन्द्रियाणां मनश्चास्मि भूतानामस्मि चेतना ॥ 22

Among the Vedas, I am the Samaveda; among the gods,
I am Vasava; among the senses, I am the mind; and among
the beings, I am consciousness.

रुद्राणां शंकरश्चास्मि वित्तेशो यक्षरक्षसाम् ।
वसूनां पावकश्चास्मि मेरुः शिखरिणामहम् ॥ 23

Of the Rudras, I am Shankara; to the trolls and demons,
I am the God of Riches; of the Vasus, I am Fire; and of the
mountains, I am Meru.

पुरोधसां च मुख्यं मां विद्धि पार्थ बृहस्पतिम् ।
सेनानीनामहं स्कन्दः सरसामस्मि सागरः ॥ 24

Of the royal priests, know me as their chief, Brihaspati. Of
the generals, I am Skanda. Of the waters, I am the ocean.

महर्षीणां भृगुरहं गिरामस्म्येकमक्षरम् ।
यज्ञानां जपयज्ञोऽस्मि स्थावराणां हिमालयः ॥ 25

Among the great sages, I am Bhrigu; of words, I am the One
Syllable; of the sacrifices, I am the silent prayer; of immovables,
I am the Himalayas.

अश्वत्थः सर्ववृक्षाणां देवर्षीणां च नारदः ।
गन्धर्वाणां चित्ररथः सिद्धानां कपिलो मुनिः ॥ 26

I am Ashvattha of all the trees, Narada among the divine
sages, Chitraratha among the Gandharvas, and the hermit
Kapila of the perfected ones.

उच्चैःश्रवसमश्वानां विद्धि माममृतोद्भवम् ।
ऐरावतं गजेन्द्राणां नराणां च नराधिपम् ॥ 27

Among horses, know me as Ucchaishravas, risen from the
nectar of immortality; as Airavata of lordly elephants; and as
the king among men.

आयुधानामहं वज्रं धेनूनामस्मि कामधुक् ।
प्रजनश्चास्मि कन्दर्पः सर्पाणामस्मि वासुकिः ॥ 28

Among weapons, I am the thunderbolt; among cows, the Cow
of Plenty; as progenitor, I am Kandarpa; and among snakes,
I am Vasuki.

अनन्तश्चास्मि नागानां वरुणो यादसामहम् ।
पितृणामर्यमा चास्मि यमः संयमतामहम् ॥ 29

Among the serpents, I am Ananta; of the sea monsters, I am
Varuna. I am Aryaman among the fathers, and Yama among
those who bind.

प्रह्लादश्चास्मि दैत्यानां कालः कलयतामहम् ।
मृगाणां च मृगेन्द्रोऽहं वैनतेयश्च पक्षिणाम् ॥ 30

I am Prahlada among the titans; I am Time among those who
impel; of animals, I am the king of animals; and of birds, I am
Garuda, the son of Vinata.

पवनः पवतामस्मि रामः शस्त्रभृतामहम् ।
झषाणां मकरश्चास्मि स्रोतसामस्मि जाह्नवी ॥ 31

Of purifiers, I am the wind; I am Rama among men of arms.
Among water monsters, I am the crocodile; and of rivers, I am
the Ganges, daughter of Jahnu.

सर्गाणामादिरन्तश्च मध्यं चैवाहमर्जुन ।
अध्यात्मविद्या विद्यानां वादः प्रवदतामहम् ॥ 32

I am the beginning, the end, and also the middle of the
creations, Arjuna. I am the wisdom of the self among all
wisdom, the argument of those who speak.

अक्षराणामकारोऽस्मि द्वंद्वः सामासिकस्य च ।
अहमेवाक्षयः कालो धाताहं विश्वतोमुखः ॥ 33

I am the letter *A* of the letters, the conjunction among the
compound words; yes, I am everlasting Time and the creator
facing all directions.

मृत्युः सर्वहरश्चाहमुद्भवश्च भविष्यताम् ।
कीर्तिः श्रीर्वाक्च नारीणां स्मृतिर्मेधा धृतिः क्षमा ॥ 34

I am all-snatching death and the origin of those about to
be. Among feminine things, I am fame, prosperity, speech,
memory, prudence, resolution, and patience.

बृहत्साम तथा साम्नां गायत्री छन्दसामहम् ।
मासानां मार्गशीर्षोऽहमृतूनां कुसुमाकरः ॥ 35

Thus, I am the High Chant among the chants, the Gayatri of the meters. Of the months, I am Margashirsha; of the seasons, spring.

द्यूतं छलयतामस्मि तेजस्तेजस्विनामहम् ।
जयोऽस्मि व्यवसायोऽस्मि सत्त्वं सत्त्ववतामहम् ॥ ३६

Of deceitful things, I am gambling; of the splendid, I am splendor. I am the victory, the resolution, the courage of the courageous.

वृष्णीनां वासुदेवोऽस्मि पाण्डवानां धनंजयः ।
मुनीनामप्यहं व्यासः कवीनामुशना कविः ॥ ३७

Among the Vrishnis, I am Vasudeva; among the Pandu sons, I am Dhananjaya; among the sages, I am Vyasa; and among the poets, I am the poet Ushanas.

दण्डो दमयतामस्मि नीतिरस्मि जिगीषताम् ।
मौनं चैवास्मि गुह्यानां ज्ञानं ज्ञानवतामहम् ॥ ३८

I am the stick of those who chastise. I am statesmanship in those who seek to conquer. I am the silence of secrets and the knowledge of the knowers.

यच्चापि सर्वभूतानां बीजं तदहमर्जुन ।
न तदस्ति विना यत्स्यान्मया भूतं चराचरम् ॥ ३९

I am also, Arjuna, whatever be the seed of all beings. No being moving or standing could exist without me.

नान्तोऽस्ति मम दिव्यानां विभूतीनां परंतप ।
एष तूद्देशतः प्रोक्तो विभूतेर्विस्तरो मया ॥ 40

There is no end to my wonderful manifestations, Scorcher of Enemies. I have merely given examples of the full extent of my manifestation.

यद्यद्विभूतिमत्सत्त्वं श्रीमदूर्जितमेव वा ।
तत्तदेवावगच्छ त्वं मम तेजोंऽशसंभवम् ॥ 41

Whatever being has power, luster, and vigor, know that its origin was a particle of my splendor.

अथ वा बहुनैतेन किं ज्ञातेन तवार्जुन ।
विष्टभ्याहमिदं कृत्स्नमेकांशेन स्थितो जगत् ॥ 42

But why do you need such detailed knowledge, Arjuna? I firmly support this whole world with but a part of myself.'

इति श्रीमहाभारते शतसाहस्रायां संहितायां श्रीमद्भगवद्गीतायां ब्रह्मविद्याशास्त्रे श्रीकृष्णार्जुनसंवादे विभूतियोगो नाम दशमोऽध्यायः ॥

Thus ends the tenth chapter, entitled "The Reflection upon Power," in the instruction which teaches the sacred knowledge given by the exalted Krishna in his conversation with Arjuna, the auspicious Bhagavad Gita, which is in the work of a hundred thousand verses, the glorious *Mahabharata*.

एकादशोऽध्यायः

Chapter Eleven

His Cosmic Form

अर्जुन उवाच ।
मदनुग्रहाय परमं गुह्यमध्यात्मसंज्ञितम् ।
यत्त्वयोक्तं वचस्तेन मोहोऽयं विगतो मम ॥ १

Arjuna said, 'The speech you have made as a favor to me about the supreme mystery of the self has dispelled my delusion.

भवाप्ययौ हि भूतानां श्रुतौ विस्तरशो मया ।
त्वत्तः कमलपत्राक्ष माहात्म्यमपि चाव्ययम् ॥ २

From you, Lotus Eyed, I have heard in detail about both the origin and the disappearance of beings, and about your imperishable greatness.

एवमेतद्यथात्थ त्वमात्मानं परमेश्वर ।
द्रष्टुमिच्छामि ते रूपमैश्वरं पुरुषोत्तम ॥ ३

Supreme Spirit, I want to see your supernal form, just as you have described yourself, Supreme Lord.

मन्यसे यदि तच्छक्यं मया द्रष्टुमिति प्रभो ।

योगेश्वर ततो मे त्वं दर्शयात्मानमव्ययम् ॥ ४

If you think it is possible for me to see you, Lord, then show
me your imperishable self, Lord of Yoga!'

श्रीभगवानुवाच ।
पश्य मे पार्थ रूपाणि शतशोऽथ सहस्रशः ।
नानाविधानि दिव्यानि नानावर्णाकृतीनि च ॥ ५

The Lord said, 'Behold my forms, Son of Pritha, by the
hundreds and the thousands, of many different kinds,
wonderful, and in various shapes and colors.

पश्यादित्यान्वसून्रुद्रानश्विनौ मरुतस्तथा ।
बहून्यदृष्टपूर्वाणि पश्याश्चर्याणि भारत ॥ ६

Behold the Adityas, the Vasus, the Rudras, the two Ashvins,
and the Maruts! Behold, Bharata, many wonders never
seen before!

इहैकस्थं जगत्कृत्स्नं पश्याद्य सचराचरम् ।
मम देहे गुडाकेश यच्चान्यद्द्रष्टुमिच्छसि ॥ ७

Behold the entire world, with beings moving and unmoving,
here unified in my body, Gudakesha, and whatever else you
want to see.

न तु मां शक्यसे द्रष्टुमनेनैव स्वचक्षुषा ।
दिव्यं ददामि ते चक्षुः पश्य मे योगमैश्वरम् ॥ ८

But you will not be able to see me with your own eyes. I give you a divine eye. Behold my superhuman magical power!'"

संजय उवाच ।
एवमुक्त्वा ततो राजन्महायोगेश्वरो हरिः ।
दर्शयामास पार्थाय परमं रूपमैश्वरम् ॥ ९
अनेकवक्त्रनयनमनेकाद्भुतदर्शनम् ।
अनेकदिव्याभरणं दिव्यानेकोद्यतायुधम् ॥ १०
दिव्यमाल्याम्बरधरं दिव्यगन्धानुलेपनम् ।
सर्वाश्चर्यमयं देवमनन्तं विश्वतोमुखम् ॥ ११

Sanjaya said, "When he had spoken thus, O King, the great Lord of Yoga, Hari, then revealed his supreme, supernal form to the son of Pritha, with its countless mouths and eyes, showing countless marvels, wearing countless divine ornaments, with countless divine weapons raised, wearing divine garlands and robes, anointed with divine perfumes and unguents—a god made of all wonders, boundless, and facing in all directions.

दिवि सूर्यसहस्रस्य भवेद्युगपदुत्थिता ।
यदि भाः सदृशी सा स्याद्भासस्तस्य महात्मनः ॥ १२

If the light of a thousand suns had risen in the sky at the same time, that would have equaled the splendor of that great soul.

तत्रैकस्थं जगत्कृत्स्नं प्रविभक्तमनेकधा ।
अपश्यद्देवदेवस्य शरीरे पाण्डवस्तदा ॥ १३

There, in the body of the god of gods, the son of Pandu
beheld the whole world, united in its infinite diversity.

ततः स विस्मयाविष्टो हृष्टरोमा धनंजयः ।
प्रणम्य शिरसा देवं कृताञ्जलिरभाषत ॥ 14

Dhananjaya, struck with amazement, his body hair bristling,
bowed his head to the god and spoke with folded hands.

अर्जुन उवाच ।
पश्यामि देवांस्तव देव देहे सर्वास्तथा भूतविशेषसंघान् ।
ब्रह्माणमीशं कमलासनस्थमृषींश्च सर्वानुरगांश्च दिव्यान् ॥ 15

Arjuna said, 'I see all the gods in your body, Lord, with the
different hosts of beings—the lord Brahma sitting on his lotus
seat, all the sages, the divine serpents.

अनेकबाहूदरवक्त्रनेत्रं पश्यामि त्वा सर्वतोऽनन्तरूपम् ।
नान्तं न मध्यं न पुनस्तवादिं पश्यामि विश्वेश्वर विश्वरूप ॥ 16

I see you with countless arms, bellies, faces, and eyes, your
form stretching endlessly in all directions. I see no end, no
middle, nor beginning of you, lord of the universe with
universal form.

किरीटिनं गदिनं चक्रिणं च तेजोराशिं सर्वतो दीप्तिमन्तम् ।
पश्यामि त्वां दुर्निरीक्ष्यं समन्तादीप्तानलार्कद्युतिमप्रमेयम् ॥ 17

I see you with your crown, your mace, and your discus;
a glowing mass shining in all directions with the splendor

of blazing fire and the sun on all sides, difficult to behold, immeasurable.

त्वमक्षरं परमं वेदितव्यं त्वमस्य विश्वस्य परं निधानम् ।
त्वमव्ययः शाश्वतधर्मगोप्ता सनातनस्त्वं पुरुषो मतो मे ॥ 18

You are the immutable, the supreme, that which should be known. You are the ultimate repository of this universe. You are the immortal guardian of the eternal law. I know you as the everlasting spirit.

अनादिमध्यान्तमनन्तवीर्यमनन्तबाहुं शशिसूर्यनेत्रम् ।
पश्यामि त्वां दीप्तहुताशवक्त्रं स्वतेजसा विश्वमिदं तपन्तम् ॥ 19

Without a beginning, a middle, or an end, with endless power, countless arms, with the moon and the sun as your eyes, I see you with your mouth as a blazing fire, burning this universe with your fiery energy.

द्यावापृथिव्योरिदमन्तरं हि व्याप्तं त्वयैकेन दिशश्च सर्वाः ।
दृष्ट्वाद्भुतं रूपमिदं तवोग्रं लोकत्रयं प्रव्यथितं महात्मन् ॥ 20

For this space between heaven and earth and all four directions is pervaded by you alone. Seeing this wondrous and terrifying form of yours, the three worlds tremble, great soul!

अमी हि त्वा सुरसंघा विशन्ति केचिद्भीताः प्राञ्जलयो गृणन्ति ।
स्वस्तीत्युक्त्वा महर्षिसिद्धसंघाः स्तुवन्ति त्वां स्तुतिभिः पुष्कलाभिः ॥ 21

For these hosts of gods enter you, and some extol you in fear with folded hands. Shouting "Hail!" the hosts of great sages and perfected ones praise you with resounding litanies.

रुद्रादित्या वसवो ये च साध्या विश्वेऽश्विनौ मरुतश्चोष्मपाश्च ।
गन्धर्वयक्षासुरसिद्धसंघा वीक्षन्ते त्वा विस्मिताश्चैव सर्वे ॥ 22

The Rudras, the Adityas, the Vasus, and the Sadhyas; the Vishvedevas, the two Ashvins, the Maruts, and the fathers; the hosts of Gandharvas, Yakshas, and perfected ones— all behold you, and are amazed.

रूपं महत्ते बहुवक्त्रनेत्रं महाबाहो बहुबाहूरुपादम् ।
बहूदरं बहुदंष्ट्राकरालं दृष्ट्वा लोकाः प्रव्यथितास्तथाहम् ॥ 23

Seeing your great form, Mighty-armed Prince, with its many mouths and eyes; its many arms, thighs, and feet; its many bellies, and dreadful with its many tusks—the worlds tremble, and so do I.

नभःस्पृशं दीप्तमनेकवर्णं व्यात्ताननं दीप्तविशालनेत्रम् ।
दृष्ट्वा हि त्वां प्रव्यथितान्तरात्मा धृतिं न विन्दामि शमं च विष्णो ॥ 24

Seeing you thus—touching the sky, blazing, with many colors, open mouth, and large, fiery eyes—my inmost self trembles, and I find neither courage nor peace, Vishnu!

दंष्ट्राकरालानि च ते मुखानि दृष्ट्वैव कालानलसंनिभानि ।
दिशो न जाने न लभे च शर्म प्रसीद देवेश जगन्निवास ॥ 25

Seeing your mouths, terrible with their tusks, like the fire
of doomsday, I lose my sense of direction and find no shelter.
Have mercy, king of the gods, home of the world!

अमी च त्वां धृतराष्ट्रस्य पुत्राः सर्वे सहैवावनिपालसंघैः ।
भीष्मो द्रोणः सूतपुत्रस्तथासौ सहास्मदीयैरपि योधमुख्यैः ॥ 26
वक्त्राणि ते त्वरमाणा विशन्ति दंष्ट्राकरालानि भयानकानि ।
केचिद्विलग्ना दशनान्तरेषु संदृश्यन्ते चूर्णितैरुत्तमाङ्गैः ॥ 27

And all these sons of Dhritarashtra, together with hosts of
kings, with Bhishma, Drona, and that son of a charioteer,
Karna, together with our best warriors, they rush into your
dreadful mouths with the terrible tusks. Some I see caught
between your teeth with their heads crushed.

यथा नदीनां बहवोऽम्बुवेगाः समुद्रमेवाभिमुखा द्रवन्ति ।
तथा तवामी नरलोकवीरा विशन्ति वक्त्राण्यभिविज्वलन्ति ॥ 28

As the many torrential waters of the rivers rush headlong into
the ocean, so these heroes of the world of men enter your
blazing mouths.

यथा प्रदीप्तं ज्वलनं पतंगा विशन्ति नाशाय समृद्धवेगाः ।
तथैव नाशाय विशन्ति लोकास्तवापि वक्त्राणि समृद्धवेगाः ॥ 29

As insects swiftly rush to their deaths in a blazing fire, in the
same way, people swiftly rush to their deaths in your mouths.

लेलिह्यसे ग्रसमानः समन्ताल्लोकान्समग्रान्वदनैर्ज्वलद्भिः ।
तेजोभिरापूर्य जगत्समग्रं भासस्तवोग्राः प्रतपन्ति विष्णो ॥ 30

Devouring all the worlds everywhere with your flaming mouths, you lick your lips eagerly. Filling the whole world with their splendor, your fierce rays burn it to a cinder, Vishnu!

आख्याहि मे को भवानुग्ररूपो नमोऽस्तु ते देववर प्रसीद ।
विज्ञातुमिच्छामि भवन्तमाद्यं न हि प्रजानामि तव प्रवृत्तिम् ॥ 31

Tell me, who are you with this terrible form? I praise you, best of gods. Show mercy! I wish to understand you, primeval Lord, for I do not comprehend your course of action.'

श्रीभगवानुवाच ।
कालोऽस्मि लोकक्षयकृत्प्रवृद्धो लोकान्समाहर्तुमिह प्रवृत्तः ।
ऋतेऽपि त्वा न भविष्यन्ति सर्वे येऽवस्थिताः प्रत्यनीकेषु योधाः ॥ 32

The Lord said, 'I am Time, full-grown destroyer of worlds, ready to annihilate these worlds. Except for you, none of the warriors arrayed in these hostile armies shall remain alive.

तस्मात्त्वमुत्तिष्ठ यशो लभस्व जित्वा शत्रून्भुङ्क्ष्व राज्यं समृद्धम् ।
मयैवैते निहताः पूर्वमेव निमित्तमात्रं भव सव्यसाचिन् ॥ 33

Therefore, you must rise and win glory! Conquer your enemies and enjoy a prosperous kingdom. These men have already been killed by me; you shall merely be my instrument, left-handed archer!

द्रोणं च भीष्मं च जयद्रथं च कर्णं तथान्यानपि योधवीरान् ।
मया हतांस्त्वं जहि मा व्यथिष्ठा युध्यस्व जेतासि रणे सपत्नान् ॥ 34

Slay Drona, Bhishma, Jayadratha, and Karna, as well as the other heroic warriors already slain by me. Do not waver! Fight! You will trounce your enemies in battle.'"

संजय उवाच ।
एतच्छ्रुत्वा वचनं केशवस्य कृताञ्जलिर्वेपमानः किरीटी ।
नमस्कृत्वा भूय एवाह कृष्णं सगद्गदं भीतभीतः प्रणम्य ॥ 35

Sanjaya said, "When he had heard these words from Keshava, the diademed Arjuna folded his hands, once again made his obeisance, and, bowing down trembling and terrorstruck, spoke to Krishna with a faltering voice.

अर्जुन उवाच ।
स्थाने हृषीकेश तव प्रकीर्त्या जगत्प्रहृष्यत्यनुरज्यते च ।
रक्षांसि भीतानि दिशो द्रवन्ति सर्वे नमस्यन्ति च सिद्धसंघाः ॥ 36

Arjuna said, 'It is right, Hrishikesha, that the world rejoices and becomes devoted when you are praised. The demons run terrified in all directions, but all the hosts of perfected ones pay homage to you.

कस्माच्च ते न नमेरन्महात्मन्गरीयसे ब्रह्मणोऽप्यादिकर्त्रे ।
अनन्त देवेश जगन्निवास त्वमक्षरं सदसत्तत्परं यत् ॥ 37

And why should they not pay homage to you, great soul, more venerable even than Brahma, the first creator? Eternal king of the gods, home of the world, you are immutable. You are being, nonbeing, and what is beyond that.

त्वमादिदेवः पुरुषः पुराणस्त्वमस्य विश्वस्य परं निधानम् ।
वेत्तासि वेद्यं च परं च धाम त्वया ततं विश्वमनन्तरूप ॥ 38

You are the first god, the ancient cosmic giant. You are the
ultimate receptacle of this universe. You are the knower, the
goal of knowledge, and the ultimate abode. The universe is
pervaded by you, god of endless form.

वायुर्यमोऽग्निर्वरुणः शशाङ्कः प्रजापतिस्त्वं प्रपितामहश्च ।
नमो नमस्तेऽस्तु सहस्रकृत्वः पुनश्च भूयोऽपि नमो नमस्ते ॥ 39

You are Vayu, Yama, Agni, Varuna, the moon, Prajapati, and
the great-grandfather. Praise, praise a thousandfold to you,
praise and praise to you again and again.

नमः पुरस्तादथ पृष्ठतस्ते नमोऽस्तु ते सर्वत एव सर्व ।
अनन्तवीर्यामितविक्रमस्त्वं सर्वं समाप्नोषि ततोऽसि सर्वः ॥ 40

Praise be to you in front and behind, praise be to you on every
side, O Everything! With infinite vigor and boundless might,
you encompass it all. Therefore you are all.

सखेति मत्वा प्रसभं यदुक्तं हे कृष्ण हे यादव हे सखेति ।
अजानता महिमानं तवेदं मया प्रमादात्प्रणयेन वापि ॥ 41

Whatever I may have said rashly, thinking of you as a friend,
saying, "Hi, Krishna," "Hi, Yadava," "Hi, friend," I spoke
in ignorance of this greatness of yours, in absentmindedness,
or in affection.

यच्चावहासार्थमसत्कृतोऽसि विहारशय्यासनभोजनेषु ।
एकोऽथ वाप्यच्युत तत्समक्षं तत्क्षामये त्वामहमप्रमेयम् ॥ 42

And if I have offended you, joking about matters of play, bed,
seating, or meals, alone or in the presence of others, Achyuta,
for that I ask your forgiveness, immeasurable one.

पितासि लोकस्य चराचरस्य त्वमस्य पूज्यश्च गुरुर्गरीयान् ।
न त्वत्समोऽस्त्यभ्यधिकः कुतोऽन्यो लोकत्रयेऽप्यप्रतिमप्रभाव ॥ 43

You are the father of the world of moving and unmoving
beings. You are its object of worship and most venerable
teacher. There is no one like you. Where could there
be another surpassing you, whose might has no equal in
the three worlds?

तस्मात्प्रणम्य प्रणिधाय कायं प्रसादये त्वामहमीशमीड्यम् ।
पितेव पुत्रस्य सखेव सख्युः प्रियः प्रियायार्हसि देव सोढुम् ॥ 44

Therefore, bowing down and prostrating my body, I propitiate
you, praiseworthy Lord. Bear with me, God, like a father with
his son, a friend with his friend, a lover with the beloved.

अदृष्टपूर्वं हृषितोऽस्मि दृष्ट्वा भयेन च प्रव्यथितं मनो मे ।
तदेव मे दर्शय देव रूपं प्रसीद देवेश जगन्निवास ॥ 45

I am thrilled to have seen what has not been seen before, but
my mind trembles with fear. Show me that familiar form,
Lord! Have mercy, king of the gods, home of the world!

किरीटिनं गदिनं चक्रहस्तमिच्छामि त्वां द्रष्टुमहं तथैव ।
तेनैव रूपेण चतुर्भुजेन सहस्रबाहो भव विश्वमूर्ते ॥ 46

I wish to see you with your diadem, your mace, with the
discus in your hand as before. Assume that four-armed form
again, thousand-armed one, you in whom the universe
is embodied.'

श्रीभगवानुवाच ।
मया प्रसन्नेन तवार्जुनेदं रूपं परं दर्शितमात्मयोगात् ।
तेजोमयं विश्वमनन्तमाद्यं यन्मे त्वदन्येन न दृष्टपूर्वम् ॥ 47

The Lord said, 'I was glad to show you through my magic
power, Arjuna, this supreme form—luminous, universal,
endless, and primeval, which no one but you has seen before.

न वेदयज्ञाध्ययनैर्न दानैर्न च क्रियाभिर्न तपोभिरुग्रैः ।
एवंरूपः शक्य अहं नृलोके द्रष्टुं त्वदन्येन कुरुप्रवीर ॥ 48

No one in the world of men but you, Hero of the Kurus, can
see me in this form, neither through the Vedas, sacrifices, or
studies, nor through gifts, religious rites, or harsh austerities.

मा ते व्यथा मा च विमूढभावो दृष्ट्वा रूपं घोरमीदृङ्ममेदम् ।
व्यपेतभीः प्रीतमनाः पुनस्त्वं तदेव मे रूपमिदं प्रपश्य ॥ 49

Do not be perturbed or bewildered by seeing this terrifying
form of mine. Your terror gone, your mind at ease, behold
again my well-known form.'"

संजय उवाच ।
इत्यर्जुनं वासुदेवस्तथोक्त्वा स्वकं रूपं दर्शयामास भूयः ।
आश्वासयामास च भीतमेनं भूत्वा पुनः सौम्यवपुर्महात्मा ॥ 50

Sanjaya said, "When Vasudeva had thus spoken to Arjuna,
he again showed him his usual form, and once more being
the great-souled friend with gentle appearance, he put
the terrified man at ease.

अर्जुन उवाच ।
दृष्ट्वेदं मानुषं रूपं तव सौम्यं जनार्दन ।
इदानीमस्मि संवृत्तः सचेताः प्रकृतिं गतः ॥ 51

Arjuna said, 'Seeing this human and gentle form of yours,
Janardana, I am now my rational self again, restored to
my normal nature.'

श्रीभगवानुवाच ।
सुदुर्दर्शमिदं रूपं दृष्टवानसि यन्मम ।
देवा अप्यस्य रूपस्य नित्यं दर्शनकाङ्क्षिणः ॥ 52

The Lord said, 'You have seen this form of mine which is
indeed hard to see. Even the gods always want to see this form.

नाहं वेदैर्न तपसा न दानेन न चेज्यया ।
शक्य एवंविधो द्रष्टुं दृष्टवानसि मां यथा ॥ 53

The Vedas, austerities, gifts, or sacrifice will not make it
possible to see me like this as you have seen me.

भक्त्या त्वनन्यया शक्य अहमेवंविधोऽर्जुन ।
ज्ञातुं द्रष्टुं च तत्त्वेन प्रवेष्टुं च परंतप ॥ 54

But with exclusive devotion, I can be known truly, seen thus, and entered into, Scorcher of Enemies.

मत्कर्मकृन्मत्परमो मद्भक्तः सङ्गवर्जितः ।
निर्वैरः सर्वभूतेषु यः स मामेति पाण्डव ॥ 55

He whose actions are for me, who sees me as his goal, is devoted to me, is without attachment, and is without animosity toward any being—he comes to me, Son of Pandu.'

इति श्रीमहाभारते शतसाहस्रायां संहितायां श्रीमद्भगवद्गीतायां ब्रह्मविद्या-
शास्त्रे श्रीकृष्णार्जुनसंवादे विश्वरूपदर्शनयोगो नामैकादशोऽध्यायः ॥

Thus ends the eleventh chapter, entitled "The Reflection upon the Appearance of the Cosmic Form," in the instruction which teaches the sacred knowledge given by the exalted Krishna in his conversation with Arjuna, the auspicious Bhagavad Gita, which is in the work of a hundred thousand verses, the glorious *Mahabharata*.

द्वादशोऽध्यायः

Chapter Twelve

Devotion

अर्जुन उवाच ।
एवं सततयुक्ता ये भक्तास्त्वां पर्युपासते ।
ये चाप्यक्षरमव्यक्तं तेषां के योगवित्तमाः ॥ 1

Arjuna said, 'Of those devotees who worship you, always disciplined in this way, and of those who worship the immutable
unmanifest, which has the greatest knowledge of Yoga?'

श्रीभगवानुवाच ।
मय्यावेश्य मनो ये मां नित्ययुक्ता उपासते ।
श्रद्धया परयोपेतास्ते मे युक्ततमा मताः ॥ 2

The Lord said, 'Those who fix their minds on me and worship
me with unflinching discipline and complete faith, them I
regard as the most disciplined.

ये त्वक्षरमनिर्देश्यमव्यक्तं पर्युपासते ।
सर्वत्रगमचिन्त्यं च कूटस्थमचलं ध्रुवम् ॥ 3
संनियम्येन्द्रियग्रामं सर्वत्र समबुद्धयः ।
ते प्राप्नुवन्ति मामेव सर्वभूतहिते रताः ॥ 4

But those who worship the immutable, the undefinable, the unmanifest, the omnipresent, the inconceivable, the unchangeable, the immovable, and the fixed by controlling their senses with the same attitude in all matters, they, rejoicing in the well-being of all beings, come to me indeed.

क्लेशोऽधिकतरस्तेषामव्यक्तासक्तचेतसाम् ।
अव्यक्ता हि गतिर्दुःखं देहवद्भिरवाप्यते ॥ ५

The exertion of those whose minds are attached to the unmanifest is greater, for the unmanifest state is difficult to reach by embodied beings.

ये तु सर्वाणि कर्माणि मयि संन्यस्य मत्पराः ।
अनन्येनैव योगेन मां ध्यायन्त उपासते ॥ ६
तेषामहं समुद्धर्ता मृत्युसंसारसागरात् ।
भवामि नचिरात्पार्थ मय्यावेशितचेतसाम् ॥ ७

But those who surrender all their actions to me, are intent on me, and meditate reverently on me with unswerving Yoga, these I will soon pluck from the ocean of death and rebirth, Son of Pritha, for their minds have melded with me.

मय्येव मन आधत्स्व मयि बुद्धिं निवेशय ।
निवसिष्यसि मय्येव अत ऊर्ध्वं न संशयः ॥ ८

Fix your mind on me alone, bury your intellect in me, and in me you shall dwell thereafter, without a doubt.

अथ चित्तं समाधातुं न शक्नोषि मयि स्थिरम् ।

अभ्यासयोगेन ततो मामिच्छासुं धनंजय ॥ ९

If you cannot concentrate your thoughts firmly on me,
then try to reach me through the discipline of regular
practice, Dhananjaya.

अभ्यासेऽप्यसमर्थोऽसि मत्कर्मपरमो भव ।
मदर्थमपि कर्माणि कुर्वन्सिद्धिमवाप्स्यसि ॥ १०

But if you are unable to practice regularly, make acting for
me your highest aim. You will also reach perfection by performing actions for my sake.

अथैतदप्यशक्तोऽसि कर्तुं मद्योगमाश्रितः ।
सर्वकर्मफलत्यागं ततः कुरु यतात्मवान् ॥ ११

And if you are unable to do even this, then rely on devotion
to me and relinquish the fruits of all actions with your
self controlled.

श्रेयो हि ज्ञानमभ्यासाज्ज्ञानाद्ध्यानं विशिष्यते ।
ध्यानात्कर्मफलत्यागस्त्यागाच्छान्तिरनन्तरम् ॥ १२

For knowledge is better than practice, meditation is better
than knowledge, and relinquishment of the fruits of action
is better than meditation. Upon relinquishment comes
immediate peace.

अद्वेष्टा सर्वभूतानां मैत्रः करुण एव च ।
निर्ममो निरहंकारः समदुःखसुखः क्षमी ॥ १३

संतुष्टः सततं योगी यतात्मा दृढनिश्चयः ।
मय्यर्पितमनोबुद्धिर्यो मद्भक्तः स मे प्रियः ॥ 14

The man devoted to me, with malice toward none, friendly
and compassionate, nonpossessive, without ego-consciousness,
feeling the same about pleasure and pain, patient, always
content, a yogi, his self controlled, his resolve firm, and with
his intellect and mind fixed on me, he is dear to me.

यस्मान्नोद्विजते लोको लोकान्नोद्विजते च यः ।
हर्षामर्षभयोद्वेगैर्मुक्तो यः स च मे प्रियः ॥ 15

He whom the world does not vex, and who does not vex the
world, who is free from joy and anger, fear and vexation, he is
dear to me.

अनपेक्षः शुचिर्दक्ष उदासीनो गतव्यथः ।
सर्वारम्भपरित्यागी यो मद्भक्तः स मे प्रियः ॥ 16

The man devoted to me who is impartial, incorruptible,
capable, uninvolved, untroubled, and who relinquishes all
self-interested undertakings, he is dear to me.

यो न हृष्यति न द्वेष्टि न शोचति न काङ्क्षति ।
शुभाशुभपरित्यागी भक्तिमान्यः स मे प्रियः ॥ 17

The devotee who neither rejoices nor hates nor mourns nor
desires, relinquishing good and evil, he is dear to me.

समः शत्रौ च मित्रे च तथा मानावमानयोः ।

शीतोष्णसुखदुःखेषु समः सङ्गविवर्जितः ॥ 18
तुल्यनिन्दास्तुतिर्मौनी संतुष्टो येन केनचित् ।
अनिकेतः स्थिरमतिर्भक्तिमान्मे प्रियो नरः ॥ 19

The devotee who is the same to enemy and ally, in honor or
dishonor, the same in heat or cold, pleasure or pain, free from
attachment, indifferent to praise and blame, taciturn, content
with anything, homeless, with a steady mind—that man is
dear to me.

ये तु धर्म्यामृतमिदं यथोक्तं पर्युपासते ।
श्रद्दधाना मत्परमा भक्तास्तेऽतीव मे प्रियाः ॥ 20

Those who worship this nectar of the law as it has been
explained, these faithful devotees who see me as their goal are
very, very dear to me.'

इति श्रीमहाभारते शतसाहस्रायां संहितायां श्रीमद्भगवद्गीतायां
ब्रह्मविद्याशास्त्रे श्रीकृष्णार्जुनसंवादे भक्तियोगो नाम द्वादशोऽध्यायः ॥

Thus ends the twelfth chapter, entitled "The Reflection
upon Devotion," in the instruction which teaches the sacred
knowledge given by the exalted Krishna in his conversation
with Arjuna, the auspicious Bhagavad Gita, which is in the
work of a hundred thousand verses, the glorious *Mahabharata*.

The Field
and Its Knower

श्रीभगवानुवाच ।
इदं शरीरं कौन्तेय क्षेत्रमित्यभिधीयते ।
एतद्यो वेत्ति तं प्राहुः क्षेत्रज्ञ इति तद्विदः ॥ 1

The Lord said, 'This body, Son of Kunti, is called "the field."
He who knows this, the experts call "the knower of the field."

क्षेत्रज्ञं चापि मां विद्धि सर्वक्षेत्रेषु भारत ।
क्षेत्रक्षेत्रज्ञयोर्ज्ञानं यत्तज्ज्ञानं मतं मम ॥ 2

And know that I am the knower of the field in all fields,
Bharata! It is knowledge of the field and its knower that I
regard as real knowledge.

तत्क्षेत्रं यच्च यादृक्च यद्विकारि यतश्च यत् ।
स च यो यत्प्रभावश्च तत्समासेन मे शृणु ॥ 3

Let me summarize for you what that field is, of what kind it is, how it evolves and from what, who the knower is, and what power he has.

ऋषिभिर्बहुधा गीतं छन्दोभिर्विविधैः पृथक् ।
ब्रह्मसूत्रपदैश्चैव हेतुमद्भिर्विनिश्चितैः ॥ ४

The sages have sung about it repeatedly and variously in different Vedic hymns, and discussed it conclusively in the statements of the Brahma Sutras accompanied by arguments.

महाभूतान्यहंकारो बुद्धिरव्यक्तमेव च ।
इन्द्रियाणि दशैकं च पञ्च चेन्द्रियगोचराः ॥ ५
इच्छा द्वेषः सुखं दुःखं संघातश्चेतना धृतिः ।
एतत्क्षेत्रं समासेन सविकारमुदाहृतम् ॥ ६

The gross elements, ego-consciousness, the intellect, the unmanifest, the ten senses and the mind, the five objects of the senses, attraction, aversion, pleasure, pain, the combination of body and senses, consciousness, and endurance: This summarizes the field with its derivatives.

अमानित्वमदम्भित्वमहिंसा क्षान्तिरार्जवम् ।
आचार्योपासनं शौचं स्थैर्यमात्मविनिग्रहः ॥ ७
इन्द्रियार्थेषु वैराग्यमनहंकार एव च ।
जन्ममृत्युजराव्याधिदुःखदोषानुदर्शनम् ॥ ८
असक्तिरनभिष्वङ्गः पुत्रदारगृहादिषु ।
नित्यं च समचित्तत्वमिष्टानिष्टोपपत्तिषु ॥ ९
मयि चानन्ययोगेन भक्तिरव्यभिचारिणी ।

विविक्तदेशसेवित्वमरतिर्जनसंसदि ॥ 10
अध्यात्मज्ञाननित्यत्वं तत्त्वज्ञानार्थदर्शनम् ।
एतज्ज्ञानमिति प्रोक्तमज्ञानं यदतोऽन्यथा ॥ 11

Modesty, sincerity, nonviolence, patience, honesty, respect for
one's teacher, integrity, firmness, self-control, nonattachment
to sense objects, as well as absence of ego-consciousness;
consideration for the problems stemming from birth, death,
old age, sickness, and unhappiness; detachment from worldly
passions, not clinging to children, wife, home, etc., constant
equanimity whether pleasant or unpleasant events occur,
unswerving devotion to me through undistracted Yoga,
resorting to solitary places, shunning a crowd, constancy
in the knowledge of the self, and understanding of the aim
of knowing the truth—this is called "knowledge." What is
different from this is ignorance.

ज्ञेयं यत्तत्प्रवक्ष्यामि यज्ज्ञात्वामृतमश्नुते ।
अनादिमत्परं ब्रह्म न सत्तन्नासदुच्यते ॥ 12

I will describe what should be known, and by knowing
which, one achieves immortality: the beginningless, supreme
Brahman, said to be neither existent nor nonexistent.

सर्वतःपाणिपादं तत्सर्वतोऽक्षिशिरोमुखम् ।
सर्वतःश्रुतिमल्लोके सर्वमावृत्य तिष्ठति ॥ 13

With its hands and feet everywhere, with its eyes, head, and
mouth everywhere, with its ears everywhere, it envelops
everything in the world.

सर्वेन्द्रियगुणाभासं सर्वेन्द्रियविवर्जितम् ।
असक्तं सर्वभृच्चैव निर्गुणं गुणभोक्तृ च ॥ 14
बहिरन्तश्च भूतानामचरं चरमेव च ।
सूक्ष्मत्वात्तदविज्ञेयं दूरस्थं चान्तिके च तत् ॥ 15
अविभक्तं च भूतेषु विभक्तमिव च स्थितम् ।
भूतभर्तृ च तज्ज्ञेयं ग्रसिष्णु प्रभविष्णु च ॥ 16
ज्योतिषामपि तज्ज्योतिस्तमसः परमुच्यते ।
ज्ञानं ज्ञेयं ज्ञानगम्यं हृदि सर्वस्य विष्ठितम् ॥ 17

It appears to have the properties of all the senses while being
without them all, unattached yet all-sustaining, property-
less yet experiencing the properties, outside and inside of
beings, standing as well as moving, too subtle to be known,
far away and yet in your vicinity, undistributed although it
appears to be distributed among beings, and it should be
known as the preserver of beings as well as their devourer
and progenitor: This is the light of lights, said to be beyond
darkness, knowledge, the object of knowledge, and the goal of
knowledge, residing in everyone's heart.

इति क्षेत्रं तथा ज्ञानं ज्ञेयं चोक्तं समासतः ।
मद्भक्त एतद्विज्ञाय मद्भावायोपपद्यते ॥ 18

Thus the field, knowledge, and the object of knowledge have
been briefly described. Through this knowledge, my devotee
becomes fit for my state of being.

प्रकृतिं पुरुषं चैव विद्ध्यनादी उभावपि ।
विकारांश्च गुणांश्चैव विद्धि प्रकृतिसंभवान् ॥ 19

Know that primordial nature and the spirit are both without beginning, and know that the derivatives and properties have their origin in primordial nature.

कार्यकारणकर्तृत्वे हेतुः प्रकृतिरुच्यते ।
पुरुषः सुखदुःखानां भोक्तृत्वे हेतुरुच्यते ॥ 20

Primordial nature is said to be the impulse for agency, cause, and effects. The spirit is said to be the cause in the experience of pleasure and pain.

पुरुषः प्रकृतिस्थो हि भुङ्क्ते प्रकृतिजान्गुणान् ।
कारणं गुणसङ्गोऽस्य सदसद्योनिजन्मसु ॥ 21

For the spirit, residing in primordial nature, experiences the properties springing from primordial nature. Its association with the properties is the cause of births in good or bad wombs.

उपद्रष्टानुमन्ता च भर्ता भोक्ता महेश्वरः ।
परमात्मेति चाप्युक्तो देहेऽस्मिन्पुरुषः परः ॥ 22

Spectator and consenter, sustainer, experiencer, great lord, and supreme self: Thus is called the supreme spirit in this body.

य एवं वेत्ति पुरुषं प्रकृतिं च गुणैः सह ।
सर्वथा वर्तमानोऽपि न स भूयोऽभिजायते ॥ 23

He who knows the spirit and primordial nature with its properties in this manner, he will not be born again, however he now exists.

ध्यानेनात्मनि पश्यन्ति केचिदात्मानमात्मना ।
अन्ये सांख्येन योगेन कर्मयोगेन चापरे ॥ 24

Some see the self by the self in the self through meditation, others through theoretical discipline, others through the discipline of action.

अन्ये त्वेवमजानन्तः श्रुत्वान्येभ्य उपासते ।
तेऽपि चातितरन्त्येव मृत्युं श्रुतिपरायणाः ॥ 25

But others, who are ignorant of this, hear it from others and worship, and these too, escape death in their devotion to revelation.

यावत्संजायते किंचित्सत्त्वं स्थावरजङ्गमम् ।
क्षेत्रक्षेत्रज्ञसंयोगात्तद्विद्धि भरतर्षभ ॥ 26

When a being, moving or standing, is born, know that this is due to the union of the field and the knower of the field, Bull of the Bharatas.

समं सर्वेषु भूतेषु तिष्ठन्तं परमेश्वरम् ।
विनश्यत्स्वविनश्यन्तं यः पश्यति स पश्यति ॥ 27

He who sees the supreme lord equally present in all beings, not perishing while they perish, he sees indeed.

समं पश्यन्हि सर्वत्र समवस्थितमीश्वरम् ।
न हिनस्त्यात्मनात्मानं ततो याति परां गतिम् ॥ 28

For seeing the lord established equally everywhere, he does not hurt his self by his self, but reaches the highest state.

प्रकृत्यैव च कर्माणि क्रियमाणानि सर्वशः ।
यः पश्यति तथात्मानमकर्तारं स पश्यति ॥ 29

He who sees that actions are always performed by primordial nature alone, and that the self does not act, he sees indeed.

यदा भूतपृथग्भावमेकस्थमनुपश्यति ।
तत एव च विस्तारं ब्रह्म संपद्यते तदा ॥ 30

When he sees that the distinctness of beings has its base in the One and spreads from there, he attains Brahman.

अनादित्वान्निर्गुणत्वात्परमात्मायमव्ययः ।
शरीरस्थोऽपि कौन्तेय न करोति न लिप्यते ॥ 31

This supreme self is imperishable because it has no beginning and no properties. Although it resides in the body, Son of Kunti, it does not act, nor is it defiled.

यथा सर्वगतं सौक्ष्म्यादाकाशं नोपलिप्यते ।
सर्वत्रावस्थितो देहे तथात्मा नोपलिप्यते ॥ 32

Just as all-pervading space is not defiled because it is so subtle, thus the self, although present in every body, is not defiled.

यथा प्रकाशयत्येकः कृत्स्नं लोकमिमं रविः ।
क्षेत्रं क्षेत्री तथा कृत्स्नं प्रकाशयति भारत ॥ 33

Just as one sun illumines this whole world, so the lord of the field illumines the whole field, Bharata.

क्षेत्रक्षेत्रज्ञयोरेवमन्तरं ज्ञानचक्षुषा ।
भूतप्रकृतिमोक्षं च ये विदुर्यान्ति ते परम् ॥ 34

Those who know, through their eye of knowledge, the distinction between the field and the knower of the field, and the release of beings from primordial nature—they reach the Supreme.'

इति श्रीमहाभारते शतसाहस्रायां संहितायां श्रीमद्भगवद्गीतायां ब्रह्मविद्या-
शास्त्रे श्रीकृष्णार्जुनसंवादे क्षेत्रक्षेत्रज्ञयोगाख्यस्त्रयोदशोऽध्यायः ॥

Thus ends the thirteenth chapter, entitled "The Reflection upon the Field and the Knower of the Field," in the instruction which teaches the sacred knowledge given by the exalted Krishna in his conversation with Arjuna, the auspicious Bhagavad Gita, which is in the work of a hundred thousand verses, the glorious *Mahabharata*.

Chapter Fourteen

The Three Properties

श्रीभगवानुवाच ।
परं भूयः प्रवक्ष्यामि ज्ञानानां ज्ञानमुत्तमम् ।
यज्ज्ञात्वा मुनयः सर्वे परां सिद्धिमितो गताः ॥ 1

The Lord said, 'I will explain again the ultimate and highest knowledge of all knowledge, through which all sages have gone from this world to supreme perfection.

इदं ज्ञानमुपाश्रित्य मम साधर्म्यमागताः ।
सर्गेऽपि नोपजायन्ते प्रलये न व्यथन्ति च ॥ 2

By resorting to this knowledge, they have achieved the same nature as me. They are not born at the time of creation, nor are they disturbed at the time of dissolution.

मम योनिर्महद्ब्रह्म तस्मिन्गर्भं दधाम्यहम् ।
संभवः सर्वभूतानां ततो भवति भारत ॥ 3

The great Brahman is my womb. In this I put an embryo. From this all beings have their origin, Bharata.

सर्वयोनिषु कौन्तेय मूर्तयः संभवन्ति याः ।
तासां ब्रह्म महद्योनिरहं बीजप्रदः पिता ॥ 4

Great Brahman is the womb of all wombs in which forms are
produced, Son of Kunti. I am the father giving the seed.

सत्त्वं रजस्तम इति गुणाः प्रकृतिसंभवाः ।
निबध्नन्ति महाबाहो देहे देहिनमव्ययम् ॥ 5

Clarity, agitation, and sluggishness: These properties, born
of primordial nature, bind the imperishable embodied soul in
the body, Mighty-armed Prince.

तत्र सत्त्वं निर्मलत्वात्प्रकाशकमनामयम् ।
सुखसङ्गेन बध्नाति ज्ञानसङ्गेन चानघ ॥ 6

Among these properties, clarity causes illumination and good
health because it is pure. It binds the soul through attachment
to joy and knowledge, blameless Prince.

रजो रागात्मकं विद्धि तृष्णासङ्गसमुद्भवम् ।
तन्निबध्नाति कौन्तेय कर्मसङ्गेन देहिनम् ॥ 7

Know that agitation is characterized by passion, which
arises from attachment to desire. It binds the embodied soul
through attachment to action, Son of Kunti.

तमस्त्वज्ञानजं विद्धि मोहनं सर्वदेहिनाम् ।
प्रमादालस्यनिद्राभिस्तन्निबध्नाति भारत ॥ 8

And know that sluggishness, born of ignorance, deludes all embodied souls. It binds through negligence, sloth, and sleep, Bharata.

सत्त्वं सुखे सञ्जयति रजः कर्मणि भारत ।
ज्ञानमावृत्य तु तमः प्रमादे सञ्जयत्युत ॥ 9

Clarity attaches one to joy, agitation to action, Bharata. But sluggishness, veiling knowledge, attaches one to negligence.

रजस्तमश्चाभिभूय सत्त्वं भवति भारत ।
रजः सत्त्वं तमश्चैव तमः सत्त्वं रजस्तथा ॥ 10

Clarity prevails by overpowering agitation and sluggishness, Bharata, agitation by overpowering clarity and sluggishness, and sluggishness by overpowering clarity and agitation.

सर्वद्वारेषु देहेऽस्मिन्प्रकाश उपजायते ।
ज्ञानं यदा तदा विद्याद्विवृद्धं सत्त्वमित्युत ॥ 11

When knowledge shines forth as light through all the gates in this body, then one should know that this means an increase in clarity.

लोभः प्रवृत्तिरारम्भः कर्मणामशमः स्पृहा ।
रजस्येतानि जायन्ते विवृद्धे भरतर्षभ ॥ 12

Greed, activity, taking on projects, restlessness, desire: These arise when agitation increases, Bull of the Bharatas.

अप्रकाशोऽप्रवृत्तिश्च प्रमादो मोह एव च ।
तमस्येतानि जायन्ते विवृद्धे कुरुनन्दन ॥ 13

Obscurity, inactivity, negligence, and indeed, delusion: These
arise when sluggishness increases, Joy of the Kurus.

यदा सत्त्वे प्रवृद्धे तु प्रलयं याति देहभृत् ।
तदोत्तमविदां लोकानमलान्प्रतिपद्यते ॥ 14

If the embodied soul meets dissolution when clarity
prevails, then it attains the pure worlds of those who have
supreme knowledge.

रजसि प्रलयं गत्वा कर्मसङ्गिषु जायते ।
तथा प्रलीनस्तमसि मूढयोनिषु जायते ॥ 15

If it meets dissolution when agitation prevails, it is born
among people attached to action. And if it dies when sluggishness prevails, it is born in the wombs of the deluded.

कर्मणः सुकृतस्याहुः सात्त्विकं निर्मलं फलम् ।
रजसस्तु फलं दुःखमज्ञानं तमसः फलम् ॥ 16

They say that action well done has a spotless fruit characterized by clarity, but the fruit of agitation is unhappiness, and
sluggishness has ignorance as its fruit.

सत्त्वात्संजायते ज्ञानं रजसो लोभ एव च ।
प्रमादमोहौ तमसो भवतोऽज्ञानमेव च ॥ 17

Knowledge is born of clarity, and greed indeed of agitation, just as negligence, delusion, and ignorance are born of sluggishness.

ऊर्ध्वं गच्छन्ति सत्त्वस्था मध्ये तिष्ठन्ति राजसाः ।
जघन्यगुणवृत्तस्था अधो गच्छन्ति तामसाः ॥ 18

Those who are based on clarity rise upwards, those characterized by agitation remain in the middle, whereas the sluggish, who are based on the lowest property, sink downwards.

नान्यं गुणेभ्यः कर्तारं यदा द्रष्टानुपश्यति ।
गुणेभ्यश्च परं वेत्ति मद्भावं सोऽधिगच्छति ॥ 19

When the perceptive person sees that there is no other actor than the properties—and he knows that which is beyond the properties—he attains my state of being.

गुणानेतानतीत्य त्रीन्देही देहसमुद्भवान् ।
जन्ममृत्युजरादुःखैर्विमुक्तोऽमृतमश्नुते ॥ 20

When the embodied soul has transcended these three properties, the sources of the body, it is released from birth, death, old age, and sorrow, and becomes immortal.'

अर्जुन उवाच ।
कैर्लिङ्गैस्त्रीन्गुणानेतानतीतो भवति प्रभो ।
किमाचारः कथं चैतांस्त्रीन्गुणानतिवर्तते ॥ 21

Arjuna said, 'By which marks is he who has transcended the three properties characterized, Lord? How does he behave? And how does he overcome these three properties?'

श्रीभगवानुवाच ।
प्रकाशं च प्रवृत्तिं च मोहमेव च पाण्डव ।
न द्वेष्टि संप्रवृत्तानि न निवृत्तानि काङ्क्षति ॥ 22
उदासीनवदासीनो गुणैर्यो न विचाल्यते ।
गुणा वर्तन्त इत्येव योऽवतिष्ठति नेङ्गते ॥ 23

The Lord said, 'He who does not abhor illumination, activity, or even delusion when they happen, Son of Pandu, nor desires them when they cease, who, sitting like an uninvolved king, unperturbed by the properties, holding on to the thought, "It is only the properties that are acting," he is not moved.

समदुःखसुखः स्वस्थः समलोष्टाश्मकाञ्चनः ।
तुल्यप्रियाप्रियो धीरस्तुल्यनिन्दात्मसंस्तुतिः ॥ 24
मानावमानयोस्तुल्यस्तुल्यो मित्रारिपक्षयोः ।
सर्वारम्भपरित्यागी गुणातीतः स उच्यते ॥ 25

The same in pain and joy, self-contained, regarding a lump of clay, a stone, and a piece of gold as the same, the same in pleasure and unpleasantness, firm of mind, seeing no difference between praise and blame, the same in honor and dishonor, the same to friend and foe alike, having relinquished all undertakings—he is said to have transcended the properties.

मां च योऽव्यभिचारेण भक्तियोगेन सेवते ।

स गुणान्समतीत्यैतान्ब्रह्मभूयाय कल्पते ॥ 26

He who serves me resolutely with the discipline of devotion is
fit to become Brahman by transcending these properties.

ब्रह्मणो हि प्रतिष्ठाहममृतस्याव्ययस्य च ।
शाश्वतस्य च धर्मस्य सुखस्यैकान्तिकस्य च ॥ 27

For I am the foundation of Brahman, of the immortal and the
imperishable, of the eternal law, and of absolute bliss.'

इति श्रीमहाभारते शतसाहस्रायां संहितायां श्रीमद्भगवद्गीतायां ब्रह्मविद्या-
शास्त्रे श्रीकृष्णार्जुनसंवादे गुणत्रयविभागयोगारव्यश्चतुर्दशोऽध्यायः ॥

Thus ends the fourteenth chapter, entitled "The Reflection
upon the Distinction of the Three Properties," in the instruction which teaches the sacred knowledge given by the exalted
Krishna in his conversation with Arjuna, the auspicious
Bhagavad Gita, which is in the work of a hundred thousand
verses, the glorious *Mahabharata*.

पञ्चदशोऽध्यायः

Chapter Fifteen

The Supreme Spirit

श्रीभगवानुवाच ।
ऊर्ध्वमूलमधःशाखमश्वत्थं प्राहुरव्ययम् ।
छन्दांसि यस्य पर्णानि यस्तं वेद स वेदवित् ॥ 1

The Lord said, 'They speak of Ashvattha, the imperishable pipal tree, with its roots above and its branches below, whose leaves are the hymns. He who knows it, is a knower of the Vedas.

अधश्चोर्ध्वं प्रसृतास्तस्य शाखा गुणप्रवृद्धा विषयप्रवालाः ।
अधश्च मूलान्यनुसंततानि कर्मानुबन्धीनि मनुष्यलोके ॥ 2

Its branches spread downwards and upwards, nourished by the properties, with objects as their buds. Underneath, its roots, entangled with actions, extend to the world of men.

न रूपमस्येह तथोपलभ्यते नान्तो न चादिर्न च संप्रतिष्ठा ।
अश्वत्थमेनं सुविरूढमूलमसङ्गशस्त्रेण दृढेन छित्त्वा ॥ 3
ततः पदं तत्परिमार्गितव्यं यस्मिन्गता न निवर्तन्ति भूयः ।
तमेव चाद्यं पुरुषं प्रपद्ये यतः प्रवृत्तिः प्रसृता पुराणी ॥ 4

Its form is not perceived here, nor its end, beginning, or foundation. Having cut down this deep-rooted Ashvattha tree with the mighty sword of nonattachment, one should then seek that abode whence people do not return once they have reached it, saying: "I take refuge with that primordial spirit, from whom came forth this ancient activity."

निर्मानमोहा जितसङ्गदोषा अध्यात्मनित्या विनिवृत्तकामाः ।
द्वन्द्वैर्विमुक्ताः सुखदुःखसंज्ञैर्गच्छन्त्यमूढाः पदमव्ययं तत् ॥ ५

The clearheaded attain that eternal level, free from pride and delusion, having conquered the evil of attachment, immersed in the self, their desires ended, released from the pairs of opposites marked by pleasure and pain.

न तद्भासयते सूर्यो न शशाङ्को न पावकः ।
यद्गत्वा न निवर्तन्ते तद्धाम परमं मम ॥ ६

Neither sun nor moon nor fire illumine that supreme level of mine, on reaching which people do not return.

ममैवांशो जीवलोके जीवभूतः सनातनः ।
मनःषष्ठानीन्द्रियाणि प्रकृतिस्थानि कर्षति ॥ ७

A particle of me, having become an eternal soul in the world of the living, attracts the senses (of which mind is the sixth) based in primordial nature.

शरीरं यदवाप्नोति यच्चाप्युत्क्रामतीश्वरः ।
गृहीत्वैतानि संयाति वायुर्गन्धानिवाशयात् ॥ ८

When the lord takes on a body and when he leaves it, he takes hold of them and travels on, like the wind bringing scents from their source.

श्रोत्रं चक्षुः स्पर्शनं च रसनं घ्राणमेव च ।
अधिष्ठाय मनश्चायं विषयानुपसेवते ॥ ९

Commanding hearing, sight, touch, taste, and smell, as well as the mind, he savors the objects of the senses.

उत्क्रामन्तं स्थितं वापि भुञ्जानं वा गुणान्वितम् ।
विमूढा नानुपश्यन्ति पश्यन्ति ज्ञानचक्षुषः ॥ १०

Whether he leaves or stays or experiences, accompanied by the properties, the deluded do not see him. Only those with the eye of knowledge see him.

यतन्तो योगिनश्चैनं पश्यन्त्यात्मन्यवस्थितम् ।
यतन्तोऽप्यकृतात्मानो नैनं पश्यन्त्यचेतसः ॥ ११

Yogis who make an effort see him based in the self. But the unintelligent, without mastery of the self, do not see him, even if they make an effort.

यदादित्यगतं तेजो जगद्भासयतेऽखिलम् ।
यच्चन्द्रमसि यच्चाग्नौ तत्तेजो विद्धि मामकम् ॥ १२

Know that the splendor in the sun which illumines the whole world, as well as the splendor in the moon and in fire, is mine.

गामाविश्य च भूतानि धारयाम्यहमोजसा ।
पुष्णामि चौषधीः सर्वाः सोमो भूत्वा रसात्मकः ॥ 13

I sustain beings through my power when I enter the earth. I nourish all herbs when I become the juicy soma.

अहं वैश्वानरो भूत्वा प्राणिनां देहमाश्रितः ।
प्राणापानसमायुक्तः पचाम्यन्नं चतुर्विधम् ॥ 14

Having become the digestive fire in the body of living beings, I digest the four kinds of food with the aid of inhaled and exhaled breath.

सर्वस्य चाहं हृदि संनिविष्टो मत्तः स्मृतिर्ज्ञानमपोहनं च ।
वेदैश्च सर्वैरहमेव वेद्यो वेदान्तकृद्वेदविदेव चाहम् ॥ 15

I am embedded in everyone's heart, and tradition, knowledge, and reason spring from me. I may be known through all the Vedas. I am the maker of Vedanta and the knower of the Vedas.

द्वाविमौ पुरुषौ लोके क्षरश्चाक्षर एव च ।
क्षरः सर्वाणि भूतानि कूटस्थोऽक्षर उच्यते ॥ 16

There are these two spirits in the world: the perishable and the imperishable. The perishable is all beings; the imperishable is said to be unchangeable.

उत्तमः पुरुषस्त्वन्यः परमात्मेत्युदाहृतः ।
यो लोकत्रयमाविश्य बिभर्त्यव्यय ईश्वरः ॥ 17

But there is another, highest spirit, called "the supreme self," which enters the three worlds as the imperishable lord and sustains them.

यस्मात्क्षरमतीतोऽहमक्षरादपि चोत्तमः ।
अतोऽस्मि लोके वेदे च प्रथितः पुरुषोत्तमः ॥ 18

Because I transcend the mutable and am higher than the immutable, I am celebrated in the world and in the Vedas as the supreme spirit.

यो मामेवमसंमूढो जानाति पुरुषोत्तमम् ।
स सर्वविद्भजति मां सर्वभावेन भारत ॥ 19

He who is without delusions and knows me thus as the supreme spirit, he knows it all and worships me with all his being, Bharata.

इति गुह्यतमं शास्त्रमिदमुक्तं मयानघ ।
एतद्बुद्ध्वा बुद्धिमान्स्यात्कृतकृत्यश्च भारत ॥ 20

Thus have I taught this mysterious science, blameless Prince. By understanding this, a man should become wise and achieve his purpose, Bharata.'

इति श्रीमहाभारते शतसाहस्रायां संहितायां श्रीमद्भगवद्गीतायां ब्रह्मविद्या-
शास्त्रे श्रीकृष्णार्जुनसंवादे पुरुषोत्तमयोगाख्यः पञ्चदशोऽध्यायः ॥

Thus ends the fifteenth chapter, entitled "The Reflection upon the Supreme Spirit," in the instruction which teaches the sacred knowledge given by the exalted Krishna in his conversation with Arjuna, the auspicious Bhagavad Gita, which is in the work of a hundred thousand verses, the glorious *Mahabharata*.

षोडशोऽध्यायः

Chapter Sixteen

The Divine
and the Demonic

श्रीभगवानुवाच ।
अभयं सत्त्वसंशुद्धिर्ज्ञानयोगव्यवस्थितिः ।
दानं दमश्च यज्ञश्च स्वाध्यायस्तप आर्जवम् ॥ 1
अहिंसा सत्यमक्रोधस्त्यागः शान्तिरपैशुनम् ।
दया भूतेष्वलोलुप्त्वं मार्दवं ह्रीरचापलम् ॥ 2
तेजः क्षमा धृतिः शौचमद्रोहो नातिमानिता ।
भवन्ति संपदं दैवीमभिजातस्य भारत ॥ 3

The Lord said, 'Fearlessness, purity of nature, reliance upon
the discipline of knowledge, charity, self-control, sacrifice and
Vedic study, austerity, rectitude, nonviolence, truth, freedom
from anger, relinquishment, peace, avoidance of calumny,
compassion for beings, freedom from greed, kindness,
modesty, steadiness, vigor, patience, resolution, integrity,
freedom from malice and excessive pride: These are the
qualities of one born to divine fortune, Bharata.

दम्भो दर्पोऽतिमानश्च क्रोधः पारुष्यमेव च ।

अज्ञानं चाभिजातस्य पार्थ संपदमासुरीम् ॥ ४

Deceit, arrogance, great pride, anger, harshness, and ignorance, Son of Pritha, are the qualities of one born to demonic fortune.

दैवी संपद्विमोक्षाय निबन्धायासुरी मता ।
मा शुचः संपदं दैवीमभिजातोऽसि पाण्डव ॥ ५

We know divine fortune leads to release; demonic to bondage. Do not worry, Son of Pandu. You are born to divine fortune.

द्वौ भूतसर्गौ लोकेऽस्मिन्दैव आसुर एव च ।
दैवो विस्तरशः प्रोक्त आसुरं पार्थ मे शृणु ॥ ६

Two kinds of beings have been created in this world: the divine and the demonic. I have spoken to you about the divine kind in detail. Now hear me speak about the demonic, Son of Pritha.

प्रवृत्तिं च निवृत्तिं च जना न विदुरासुराः ।
न शौचं नापि चाचारो न सत्यं तेषु विद्यते ॥ ७

Demonic people do not know when to act and when to desist from action, nor does one find integrity, good conduct, or truth in them.

असत्यमप्रतिष्ठं ते जगदाहुरनीश्वरम् ।
अपरस्परसंभूतं किमन्यत्कामहैतुकम् ॥ ८

They say the world is devoid of truth, without a foundation, without a lord, not produced through mutual causation, and even worse, caused by desire.

एतां दृष्टिमवष्टभ्य नष्टात्मानोऽल्पबुद्धयः ।
प्रभवन्त्युग्रकर्माणः क्षयाय जगतोऽहिताः ॥ 9

Holding this view, these lost souls of small intelligence fan out with cruel deeds as enemies of the world to destroy it.

काममाश्रित्य दुष्पूरं दम्भमानमदान्विताः ।
मोहाद्गृहीत्वासद्ग्राहान्प्रवर्तन्तेऽशुचिव्रताः ॥ 10

Embracing an insatiable desire, filled with hypocrisy, arrogance, and pride, in their delusion they hold false views and follow impure vows.

चिन्तामपरिमेयां च प्रलयान्तामुपाश्रिताः ।
कामोपभोगपरमा एतावदिति निश्चिताः ॥ 11
आशापाशशतैर्बद्धाः कामक्रोधपरायणाः ।
ईहन्ते कामभोगार्थमन्यायेनार्थसंचयान् ॥ 12

Subject to innumerable anxieties ending only with death, entirely devoted to indulging their desires, convinced that "this is all," bound by a hundred snares of hope, giving in to anger and desire, they strive to accumulate wealth by unjust means in order to fulfill their desires.

इदमद्य मया लब्धमिदं प्राप्स्ये मनोरथम् ।
इदमस्तीदमपि मे भविष्यति पुनर्धनम् ॥ 13

"This I have received today, this wish I will obtain later, this I have, and this wealth I'll get later.

आसौ मया हतः शत्रुर्हनिष्ये चापरानपि ।
ईश्वरोऽहमहं भोगी सिद्धोऽहं बलवान्सुखी ॥ 14

That enemy I have killed and I'll kill others as well. I am a master. I am an enjoyer. I am successful, powerful, and happy.

आढ्योऽभिजनवानस्मि कोऽन्योऽस्ति सदृशो मया ।
यक्ष्ये दास्यामि मोदिष्य इत्यज्ञानविमोहिताः ॥ 15

I am rich, of noble birth—who is my equal? I will sacrifice, I will be generous, I will be merry!" Thus they think, deluded by ignorance.

अनेकचित्तविभ्रान्ता मोहजालसमावृताः ।
प्रसक्ताः कामभोगेषु पतन्ति नरकेऽशुचौ ॥ 16

Distracted by many concerns, entangled in the snares of delusion, addicted to the gratification of desires, they fall into a foul hell.

आत्मसंभाविताः स्तब्धा धनमानमदान्विताः ।
यजन्ते नामयज्ञैस्ते दम्भेनाविधिपूर्वकम् ॥ 17

Self-conceited, puffed up, intoxicated by wealth and arrogance, they sacrifice with sacrifices that are so in name only, full of hypocrisy, and without following the proper ritual rules.

अहंकारं बलं दर्पं कामं क्रोधं च संश्रिताः ।
मामात्मपरदेहेषु प्रद्विषन्तोऽभ्यसूयकाः ॥ 18
तानहं द्विषतः क्रूरान्संसारेषु नराधमान् ।
क्षिपाम्यजस्रमशुभानासुरीष्वेव योनिषु ॥ 19

Driven by their ego-consciousness, force, arrogance, lust, and anger, maliciously hating me in their own bodies and in those of others, cruel, and the vilest of men in these cycles of life: I forever hurl these hateful people into demonic wombs, into misfortune.

आसुरीं योनिमापन्ना मूढा जन्मनि जन्मनि ।
मामप्राप्यैव कौन्तेय ततो यान्त्यधमां गतिम् ॥ 20

Entering a demonic womb, deluded birth after birth, they fail to reach me, Son of Kunti, and fall to the lowest state.

त्रिविधं नरकस्येदं द्वारं नाशनमात्मनः ।
कामः क्रोधस्तथा लोभस्तस्मादेतत्त्रयं त्यजेत् ॥ 21

This gateway to hell, leading the self to destruction, is threefold: desire, anger, and greed. Therefore one should avoid these three.

एतैर्विमुक्तः कौन्तेय तमोद्वारैस्त्रिभिर्नरः ।
आचरत्यात्मनः श्रेयस्ततो याति परां गतिम् ॥ 22

When a man has been released from these three gateways to darkness, Son of Kunti, he practices what is good for his self, and then he reaches the highest state.

यः शास्त्रविधिमुत्सृज्य वर्तते कामकारतः ।
न स सिद्धिमवाप्नोति न सुखं न परां गतिम् ॥ 23

He who discards the precepts of scripture and keeps indulging
his desires, he does not achieve perfection, nor happiness, nor
the highest state.

तस्माच्छास्त्रं प्रमाणं ते कार्याकार्यव्यवस्थितौ ।
ज्ञात्वा शास्त्रविधानोक्तं कर्म कर्तुमिहार्हसि ॥ 24

Therefore, let scripture be your authority when you establish
what you should do and not do. Once you know what is said in
the rules of scripture, you may perform actions in this world.'

इति श्रीमहाभारते शतसाहस्रायां संहितायां श्रीमद्भगवद्गीतायां
ब्रह्मविद्याशास्त्रे श्रीकृष्णार्जुनसंवादे दैवासुरसम्पद्विभागायोगाख्यः
षोडशोऽध्यायः ॥

Thus ends the sixteenth chapter, entitled "The Reflection upon
the Distinction between the Destiny of Divine and Demonic
Creation," in the instruction which teaches the sacred
knowledge given by the exalted Krishna in his conversation
with Arjuna, the auspicious Bhagavad Gita, which is in the
work of a hundred thousand verses, the glorious *Mahabharata*.

सप्तदशोऽध्यायः

Chapter Seventeen

The Three
Kinds of Faith

अर्जुन उवाच ।
ये शास्त्रविधिमुत्सृज्य यजन्ते श्रद्धयान्विताः ।
तेषां निष्ठा तु का कृष्ण सत्त्वमाहो रजस्तमः ॥ 1

Arjuna said, 'What is the condition of those who discard the precepts of scripture, yet sacrifice filled with faith, Krishna? Clarity, agitation, or sluggishness?'

श्रीभगवानुवाच ।
त्रिविधा भवति श्रद्धा देहिनां सा स्वभावजा ।
सात्त्विकी राजसी चैव तामसी चेति तां शृणु ॥ 2

The Lord said, 'The faith of embodied souls is threefold, born of their nature. It is characterized by clarity, agitation, or sluggishness. Now hear about it!

सत्त्वानुरूपा सर्वस्य श्रद्धा भवति भारत ।
श्रद्धामयोऽयं पुरुषो यो यच्छ्रद्धः स एव सः ॥ 3

Everyone's faith conforms to his nature, Bharata. This human person is made of faith. A man's faith makes him what he is.

यजन्ते सात्त्विका देवान्यक्षरक्षांसि राजसाः ।
प्रेतान्भूतगणांश्चान्ये यजन्ते तामसा जनाः ॥ ४

People characterized by clarity sacrifice to the gods, those characterized by agitation to trolls and demons, and those characterized by sluggishness sacrifice to ghosts and ghouls.

अशास्त्रविहितं घोरं तप्यन्ते ये तपो जनाः ।
दम्भाहंकारसंयुक्ताः कामरागबलान्विताः ॥ ५
कर्शयन्तः शरीरस्थं भूतग्राममचेतसः ।
मां चैवान्तःशरीरस्थं तान्विद्ध्यासुरनिश्चयान् ॥ ६

As for the people who, performing terrible austerities not ordained by scripture, full of ostentation and egotism, impelled by the force of desire and passion, mindlessly wracking the elements in their bodies, as well as me residing inside their bodies, know that their resolves are demonic.

आहारस्त्वपि सर्वस्य त्रिविधो भवति प्रियः ।
यज्ञस्तपस्तथा दानं तेषां भेदमिमं शृणु ॥ ७

Even the food that is dear to everyone is threefold, and so are their sacrifices, asceticism, and generosity. Hear about their distinctive characters.

आयुःसत्त्वबलारोग्यसुखप्रीतिविवर्धनाः ।
रस्याः स्निग्धाः स्थिरा हृद्या आहाराः सात्त्विकप्रियाः ॥ ८

Food that increases life, vigor, health, happiness, and joy, that is tasty, rich, nourishing, and savory is dear to those who are dominated by clarity.

कट्वम्ललवणात्युष्णतीक्ष्णरूक्षविदाहिनः ।
आहारा राजसस्येष्टा दुःखशोकामयप्रदाः ॥ 9

Food that is bitter, sour, salty, very hot, sharp, astringent, and pungent is popular with those who are dominated by agitation. It causes pain, grief, and disease.

यातयामं गतरसं पूति पर्युषितं च यत् ।
उच्छिष्टमपि चामेध्यं भोजनं तामसप्रियम् ॥ 10

Food that is spoiled, tasteless, foul smelling, and kept overnight, as well as polluted leftovers, is dear to those dominated by sluggishness.

अफलाकाङ्क्षिभिर्यज्ञो विधिदृष्टो य इज्यते ।
यष्टव्यमेवेति मनः समाधाय स सात्त्विकः ॥ 11

That sacrifice is dominated by clarity which is prescribed in the ritual directions and performed by men who do not seek its fruit, but have the attitude that "sacrifices simply have to be performed."

अभिसंधाय तु फलं दम्भार्थमपि चैव यत् ।
इज्यते भरतश्रेष्ठ तं यज्ञं विद्धि राजसम् ॥ 12

Know that sacrifice to be dominated by agitation which is performed with a view to the fruit and for the sake of ostentation, Best of the Bharatas.

विधिहीनमसृष्टान्नं मन्त्रहीनमदक्षिणम् ।
श्रद्धाविरहितं यज्ञं तामसं परिचक्षते ॥ 13

The sacrifice which is not based on the ritual directions, where no food is distributed, where no Vedic hymns are chanted, where no sacrificial fee is paid, and which is performed without faith, that sacrifice is said to be dominated by sluggishness.

देवद्विजगुरुप्राज्ञपूजनं शौचमार्जवम् ।
ब्रह्मचर्यमहिंसा च शारीरं तप उच्यते ॥ 14

Homage to gods, Brahmins, teachers, and wise men, integrity, rectitude, celibacy, and nonviolence is called austerity of the body.

अनुद्वेगकरं वाक्यं सत्यं प्रियहितं च यत् ।
स्वाध्यायाभ्यसनं चैव वाङ्मयं तप उच्यते ॥ 15

Speech which does not cause distress, which is truthful, pleasant, and beneficial, as well as the regular recitation of the Vedas is called austerity of the voice.

मनःप्रसादः सौम्यत्वं मौनमात्मविनिग्रहः ।
भावसंशुद्धिरित्येतत्तपो मानसमुच्यते ॥ 16

Serenity of mind, gentleness, silence, self-control, inner
purity: This is called austerity of the mind.

श्रद्धया परया तप्तं तपस्तत्त्रिविधं नरैः ।
अफलाकाङ्क्षिभिर्युक्तैः सात्त्विकं परिचक्षते ॥ 17

They say that this threefold austerity, practiced with the
utmost faith by disciplined men not seeking its fruits, is
dominated by clarity.

सत्कारमानपूजार्थं तपो दम्भेन चैव यत् ।
क्रियते तदिह प्रोक्तं राजसं चलमध्रुवम् ॥ 18

Austerity that is performed ostentatiously to gain honor,
respect, and reverence—that, in this world, is said to be
dominated by agitation. It is unstable and impermanent.

मूढग्राहेणात्मनो यत्पीडया क्रियते तपः ।
परस्योत्सादनार्थं वा तत्तामसमुदाहृतम् ॥ 19

Austerity that is performed with foolish notions, with self-
torture, or in order to destroy another—that is said to be
dominated by sluggishness.

दातव्यमिति यद्दानं दीयतेऽनुपकारिणे ।
देशे काले च पात्रे च तद्दानं सात्त्विकं स्मृतम् ॥ 20

A gift that is given to someone who may not reciprocate, for
the simple reason that it should be given at the right place, at

the right time, and to a worthy person, that gift is regarded as dominated by clarity.

यत्तु प्रत्युपकारार्थं फलमुद्दिश्य वा पुनः ।
दीयते च परिक्लिष्टं तद्दानं राजसं स्मृतम् ॥ 21

But the gift that is given for the sake of repayment, with an eye to the fruit, or is given reluctantly, that gift is regarded as dominated by agitation.

अदेशकाले यद्दानमपात्रेभ्यश्च दीयते ।
असत्कृतमवज्ञातं तत्तामसमुदाहृतम् ॥ 22

A gift that is given at the wrong place and time, to unworthy recipients, and without proper respect or with contempt, that gift is regarded as dominated by sluggishness.

ओं तत्सदिति निर्देशो ब्रह्मणस्त्रिविधः स्मृतः ।
ब्राह्मणास्तेन वेदाश्च यज्ञाश्च विहिताः पुरा ॥ 23

The traditional threefold designation of Brahman is "om tat sat." With this, the Brahmins, the Vedas, and the sacrifices were ordained in ancient times.

तस्मादोमित्युदाहृत्य यज्ञदानतपःक्रियाः ।
प्रवर्तन्ते विधानोक्ताः सततं ब्रह्मवादिनाम् ॥ 24

Therefore, the sacrifices, gifts, and austerities mentioned in the precepts and performed by the experts on Brahman, always start with the exclamation "om."

तदित्यनभिसंधाय फलं यज्ञतपःक्रियाः ।
दानक्रियाश्च विविधाः क्रियन्ते मोक्षकाङ्क्षिभिः ॥ 25

Men who seek release perform the various acts of sacrifice and
austerity, as well as acts of generosity, with the word "tat"
and with no thought for the fruit.

सद्भावे साधुभावे च सदित्येतत्प्रयुज्यते ।
प्रशस्ते कर्मणि तथा सच्छब्दः पार्थ युज्यते ॥ 26

The word "sat" is used when something is good and true.
In the same way, Son of Pritha, the word "sat" is used in
connection with a laudable act.

यज्ञे तपसि दाने च स्थितिः सदिति चोच्यते ।
कर्म चैव तदर्थीयं सदित्येवाभिधीयते ॥ 27

A continuous effort in sacrifice, austerity, and generosity is
said to be "sat," and action undertaken for that end is also
called "sat."

अश्रद्धया हुतं दत्तं तपस्तप्तं कृतं च यत् ।
असदित्युच्यते पार्थ न च तत्प्रेत्य नो इह ॥ 28

The oblation that is offered, the gift that is given, the austerity
that is suffered, or the action that is performed without faith
is said to be "asat," Son of Pritha. It is of no consequence in
this world or the next.'

इति श्रीमहाभारते शतसाहस्रायां संहितायां श्रीमद्भगवद्गीतायां ब्रह्मविद्या-

शास्त्रे श्रीकृष्णार्जुनसंवादे श्रद्धात्रयविभागयोगाख्यः सप्तदशोऽध्यायः ॥

Thus ends the seventeenth chapter, entitled "The Reflection upon the Distinction between the Three Kinds of Faith," in the instruction which teaches the sacred knowledge given by the exalted Krishna in his conversation with Arjuna, the auspicious Bhagavad Gita, which is in the work of a hundred thousand verses, the glorious *Mahabharata*.

Chapter Eighteen

Liberation
and Renunciation

अर्जुन उवाच ।
संन्यासस्य महाबाहो तत्त्वमिच्छामि वेदितुम् ।
त्यागस्य च हृषीकेश पृथक्केशिनिषूदन ॥ 1

Arjuna said, 'Mighty-armed Prince, I want to know the truth about renunciation, Hrishikesha, and about relinquishment, each explained separately, Slayer of Keshin.'

श्रीभगवानुवाच ।
काम्यानां कर्मणां न्यासं संन्यासं कवयो विदुः ।
सर्वकर्मफलत्यागं प्राहुस्त्यागं विचक्षणाः ॥ 2

The Lord said, 'Wise men know renunciation as the rejection of agreeable actions. The clear-sighted call relinquishment the abandonment of all the fruits of action.

त्याज्यं दोषवदित्येके कर्म प्राहुर्मनीषिणः ।
यज्ञदानतपःकर्म न त्याज्यमिति चापरे ॥ 3

Some wise men say that action should be relinquished because it is tainted, while others say that acts of sacrifice, generosity, and austerity should not be relinquished.

निश्चयं शृणु मे तत्र त्यागे भरतसत्तम ।
त्यागो हि पुरुषव्याघ्र त्रिविधः संप्रकीर्तितः ॥ ४

Listen now to my verdict on relinquishment, Best of the Bharatas. Relinquishment is said to be threefold, you tiger among men.

यज्ञदानतपःकर्म न त्याज्यं कार्यमेव तत् ।
यज्ञो दानं तपश्चैव पावनानि मनीषिणाम् ॥ ५

Acts of sacrifice, generosity, and austerity should not be relinquished; to the contrary, they should be performed. Sacrifice, generosity, and austerity purify the wise.

एतान्यपि तु कर्माणि सङ्गं त्यक्त्वा फलानि च ।
कर्तव्यानीति मे पार्थ निश्चितं मतमुत्तमम् ॥ ६

But my firm and definite opinion, Son of Pritha, is that these actions should be performed while relinquishing attachment to them and their fruits.

नियतस्य तु संन्यासः कर्मणो नोपपद्यते ।
मोहात्तस्य परित्यागस्तामसः परिकीर्तितः ॥ ७

Renunciation of a prescribed action is not right. Relinquishment of such an action is caused by confusion, and is declared to be dominated by sluggishness.

दुःखमित्येव यत्कर्म कायक्लेशभयात्त्यजेत् ।
स कृत्वा राजसं त्यागं नैव त्यागफलं लभेत् ॥ ८

If a man should relinquish an action out of fear of physical hardship, thinking it unpleasant, his relinquishment would be dominated by agitation, and it would not bring him any fruit.

कार्यमित्येव यत्कर्म नियतं क्रियतेऽर्जुन ।
सङ्गं त्यक्त्वा फलं चैव स त्यागः सात्त्विको मतः ॥ ९

A prescribed action that is performed simply because it has to be done, Arjuna, with relinquishment of attachment to it and its fruit, that relinquishment is regarded as dominated by clarity.

न द्वेष्ट्यकुशलं कर्म कुशले नानुषज्जते ।
त्यागी सत्त्वसमाविष्टो मेधावी छिन्नसंशयः ॥ १०

The wise relinquisher, suffused with clarity, who has dispelled his doubts, does not hate a disagreeable action, nor is he attached to an agreeable one.

न हि देहभृता शक्यं त्यक्तुं कर्माण्यशेषतः ।
यस्तु कर्मफलत्यागी स त्यागीत्यभिधीयते ॥ ११

For it is not possible for the embodied soul to relinquish actions completely. But one who relinquishes the fruits of action, he is indeed called a relinquisher.

अनिष्टमिष्टं मिश्रं च त्रिविधं कर्मणः फलम् ।
भवत्यत्यागिनां प्रेत्य न तु संन्यासिनां क्वचित् ॥ 12

The fruits of action in the hereafter are threefold for those who do not relinquish: agreeable, disagreeable, and mixed. But for renouncers there is none whatsoever.

पञ्चैतानि महाबाहो कारणानि निबोध मे ।
सांख्ये कृतान्ते प्रोक्तानि सिद्धये सर्वकर्मणाम् ॥ 13

Learn from me the five factors, Mighty-armed Prince, taught in the doctrine of Sankhya for the performance of all actions.

अधिष्ठानं तथा कर्ता करणं च पृथग्विधम् ।
विविधाश्च पृथक्चेष्टा दैवं चैवात्र पञ्चमम् ॥ 14

They are the substrate of action, the agent, the manifold instruments, as well as the different kinds of activities. The fifth factor is fate.

शरीरवाङ्मनोभिर्यत्कर्म प्रारभते नरः ।
न्याय्यं वा विपरीतं वा पञ्चैते तस्य हेतवः ॥ 15

The action that a man initiates with his body, voice, or mind, whether it is proper or improper, is caused by these five factors.

तत्रैवं सति कर्तारमात्मानं केवलं तु यः ।
पश्यत्यकृतबुद्धित्वान्न स पश्यति दुर्मतिः ॥ 16

This being the case, he who sees himself as the sole agent, because his intellect lacks training, is a fool and does not see at all.

यस्य नाहंकृतो भावो बुद्धिर्यस्य न लिप्यते ।
हत्वापि स इमाँल्लोकान्न हन्ति न निबध्यते ॥ 17

He whose disposition is not ego based, whose mind is not sullied, even if he kills these people, does not kill, nor is he bound.

ज्ञानं ज्ञेयं परिज्ञाता त्रिविधा कर्मचोदना ।
करणं कर्म कर्तेति त्रिविधः कर्मसंग्रहः ॥ 18

Three factors incite action: knowledge, the object of knowledge, and the knower. Action is the combined effect of three factors: the instrument, the action, and the agent.

ज्ञानं कर्म च कर्ता च त्रिधैव गुणभेदतः ।
प्रोच्यते गुणसंख्याने यथावच्छृणु तान्यपि ॥ 19

Knowledge, action, and agent are threefold according to their difference in properties. This is taught in the enumeration of properties. Duly listen to them.

सर्वभूतेषु येनैकं भावमव्ययमीक्षते ।
अविभक्तं विभक्तेषु तज्ज्ञानं विद्धि सात्त्विकम् ॥ 20

You should know that the knowledge by which a single imperishable being is perceived in all beings, undivided in the
divided, that knowledge is dominated by clarity.

पृथक्त्वेन तु यज्ज्ञानं नानाभावान्पृथग्विधान् ।
वेत्ति सर्वेषु भूतेषु तज्ज्ञानं विद्धि राजसम् ॥ 21

Know that the knowledge which sees many beings of various
kinds in all beings because they are separated, that knowledge
is dominated by agitation.

यत्तु कृत्स्नवदेकस्मिन्कार्ये सक्तमहैतुकम् ।
अतत्त्वार्थवदल्पं च तत्तामसमुदाहृतम् ॥ 22

That knowledge is said to be dominated by sluggishness which
is attached to one object as though it were the whole for no
good reason, contains no valid truth, and is trifling.

नियतं सङ्गरहितमरागद्वेषतः कृतम् ।
अफलप्रेप्सुना कर्म यत्तत्सात्त्विकमुच्यते ॥ 23

That action is said to be dominated by clarity which is obliga-
tory, devoid of attachment, and performed without love or
hatred by a person who does not wish rewards.

यत्तु कामेप्सुना कर्म साहंकारेण वा पुनः ।
क्रियते बहुलायासं तद्राजसमुदाहृतम् ॥ 24

That action is said to be dominated by agitation which is performed with much labor by a person who wishes to gratify his desires, or who acts with an egocentric attitude.

अनुबन्धं क्षयं हिंसामनपेक्ष्य च पौरुषम् ।
मोहादारभ्यते कर्म यत्तत्तामसमुच्यते ॥ 25

An action is said to be dominated by sluggishness when it is mindlessly undertaken without regard to consequences, loss, injury, and personal capacity.

मुक्तसङ्गोऽनहंवादी धृत्युत्साहसमन्वितः ।
सिद्ध्यसिद्ध्योर्निर्विकारः कर्ता सात्त्विक उच्यते ॥ 26

An agent is said to be dominated by clarity who is free from attachment, self-effacing, endowed with resolution and fortitude, and unchanged by success or failure.

रागी कर्मफलप्रेप्सुर्लुब्धो हिंसात्मकोऽशुचिः ।
हर्षशोकान्वितः कर्ता राजसः परिकीर्तितः ॥ 27

An agent is said to be dominated by agitation when he is passionate, covetous of the fruits of his actions, greedy, injurious, without integrity, and filled with joy and grief.

अयुक्तः प्राकृतः स्तब्धः शठो नैकृतिकोऽलसः ।
विषादी दीर्घसूत्री च कर्ता तामस उच्यते ॥ 28

An agent is said to be dominated by sluggishness when he is undisciplined, unrefined, stubborn, crooked, deceitful, lazy, despondent, and procrastinating.

बुद्धेर्भेदं धृतेश्चैव गुणतस्त्रिविधं शृणु ।
प्रोच्यमानमशेषेण पृथक्त्वेन धनंजय ॥ 29

Listen, Dhananjaya, to the threefold distinction of intellect and resolution according to the properties, explained wholly and severally.

प्रवृत्तिं च निवृत्तिं च कार्याकार्ये भयाभये ।
बन्धं मोक्षं च या वेत्ति बुद्धिः सा पार्थ सात्त्विकी ॥ 30

An intellect which knows activity and inactivity, what to do and what not to do, what to fear and what not to fear, what is bondage and what is release—that intellect, Son of Pritha, is dominated by clarity.

यया धर्ममधर्मं च कार्यं चाकार्यमेव च ।
अयथावत्प्रजानाति बुद्धिः सा पार्थ राजसी ॥ 31

An intellect is dominated by agitation, Son of Pritha, when it does not give correct information about what is right and what is wrong, about what should be done and not be done.

अधर्मं धर्ममिति या मन्यते तमसावृता ।
सर्वार्थान्विपरीतांश्च बुद्धिः सा पार्थ तामसी ॥ 32

An intellect is dominated by sluggishness, Son of Pritha, when it, obscured by darkness, thinks that wrong is right and turns all matters upside down.

धृत्या यया धारयते मनःप्राणेन्द्रियक्रियाः ।
योगेनाव्यभिचारिण्या धृतिः सा पार्थ सात्त्विकी ॥ 33

The resolution with which the actions of the mind, the life breath, and the senses are held by means of unswerving Yoga, that resolution, Son of Pritha, is dominated by clarity.

यया तु धर्मकामार्थान्धृत्या धारयतेऽर्जुन ।
प्रसङ्गेन फलाकाङ्क्षी धृतिः सा पार्थ राजसी ॥ 34

The resolution that makes a man eagerly pursue duty, desire, and wealth, Arjuna, wishing to enjoy their fruits, that resolution, Son of Pritha, is dominated by agitation.

यया स्वप्नं भयं शोकं विषादं मदमेव च ।
न विमुञ्चति दुर्मेधा धृतिः सा पार्थ तामसी ॥ 35

The resolution by which a fool does not cast off dreaming, fear, grief, despondency, and arrogance, that resolution, Son of Pritha, is dominated by sluggishness.

सुखं त्विदानीं त्रिविधं शृणु मे भरतर्षभ ।
अभ्यासाद्रमते यत्र दुःखान्तं च निगच्छति ॥ 36

Hear from me now, Bull of the Bharatas, of the threefold happiness, where a man comes to rest after long practice and reaches the end of his sorrows.

यत्तदग्रे विषमिव परिणामेऽमृतोपमम् ।
तत्सुखं सात्त्विकं प्रोक्तमात्मबुद्धिप्रसादजम् ॥ 37

That happiness, which is like poison in the beginning and
nectar in the end, born of the serenity in one's own mind, is
said to be dominated by clarity.

विषयेन्द्रियसंयोगाद्यत्तदग्रेऽमृतोपमम् ।
परिणामे विषमिव तत्सुखं राजसं स्मृतम् ॥ 38

The happiness which springs from the contact of senses with
sense objects, and which is like nectar in the beginning and
poison in the end, is said to be dominated by agitation.

यदग्रे चानुबन्धे च सुखं मोहनमात्मनः ।
निद्रालस्यप्रमादोत्थं तत्तामसमुदाहृतम् ॥ 39

The happiness which, in the beginning and ever after, deludes
the self, arising from dreaming, sloth, and negligence, that
happiness is said to be dominated by sluggishness.

न तदस्ति पृथिव्यां वा दिवि देवेषु वा पुनः ।
सत्त्वं प्रकृतिजैर्मुक्तं यदेभिः स्यात्त्रिभिर्गुणैः ॥ 40

There is no being on earth, nor in heaven among the gods,
who is free from these three properties springing from
primordial nature.

ब्राह्मणक्षत्रियविशां शूद्राणां च परंतप ।
कर्माणि प्रविभक्तानि स्वभावप्रभवैर्गुणैः ॥ 41

The actions of Brahmins, warriors, commoners, and serfs,
Scorcher of Enemies, are apportioned according to the properties springing from their nature.

शमो दमस्तपः शौचं क्षान्तिरार्जवमेव च ।
ज्ञानं विज्ञानमास्तिक्यं ब्रह्मकर्म स्वभावजम् ॥ 42

Tranquility, self-control, austerity, purity, patience, rectitude,
knowledge, understanding, and faith in religion are all Brahminical tasks, born of their nature.

शौर्यं तेजो धृतिर्दाक्ष्यं युद्धे चाप्यपलायनम् ।
दानमीश्वरभावश्च क्षत्रकर्म स्वभावजम् ॥ 43

Heroism, energy, resolution, capability, abstention from
retreat in battle, generosity, and the exercise of power are all
warrior tasks, born of their nature.

कृषिगोरक्ष्यवाणिज्यं वैश्यकर्म स्वभावजम् ।
परिचर्यात्मकं कर्म शूद्रस्यापि स्वभावजम् ॥ 44

Farming, cow herding, and trade are commoners' tasks, born
of their nature. The serfs' tasks, characterized by service, are
also born of their nature.

स्वे स्वे कर्मण्यभिरतः संसिद्धिं लभते नरः ।
स्वकर्मनिरतः सिद्धिं यथा विन्दति तच्छृणु ॥ 45

Men attain perfection by devoting themselves to their
separate tasks. Hear how a man devoted to his personal tasks
finds perfection.

यतः प्रवृत्तिर्भूतानां येन सर्वमिदं ततम् ।
स्वकर्मणा तमभ्यर्च्य सिद्धिं विन्दति मानवः ॥ 46

A man finds perfection by worshiping through his own work
him from whom beings have arisen, and on whom this
world is strung.

श्रेयान्स्वधर्मो विगुणः परधर्मात्स्वनुष्ठितात् ।
स्वभावनियतं कर्म कुर्वन्नाप्नोति किल्बिषम् ॥ 47

It is better to do one's own duty without distinction than
to carry out another man's duty well. He who does work
ordained by his own nature does not incur any blame.

सहजं कर्म कौन्तेय सदोषमपि न त्यजेत् ।
सर्वारम्भा हि दोषेण धूमेनाग्निरिवावृताः ॥ 48

One should not give up the work one is born to, Son of Kunti,
even if it is flawed. For all activities are clouded by flaws, just
like fire is clouded by smoke.

असक्तबुद्धिः सर्वत्र जितात्मा विगतस्पृहः ।
नैष्कर्म्यसिद्धिं परमां संन्यासेनाधिगच्छति ॥ 49

The man whose mind is not attached to anything, whose self
is conquered, his desire gone, he attains through renunciation
the ultimate perfection of freedom from karma.

सिद्धिं प्राप्तो यथा ब्रह्म तथाप्नोति निबोध मे ।
समासेनैव कौन्तेय निष्ठा ज्ञानस्य या परा ॥ 50

Hear from me briefly, Son of Kunti, how he attains Brahman,
which is the highest state of knowledge, when he has
reached perfection.

बुद्ध्या विशुद्धया युक्तो धृत्यात्मानं नियम्य च ।
शब्दादीन्विषयांस्त्यक्त्वा रागद्वेषौ व्युदस्य च ॥ 51
विविक्तसेवी लघ्वाशी यतवाक्कायमानसः ।
ध्यानयोगपरो नित्यं वैराग्यं समुपाश्रितः ॥ 52
अहंकारं बलं दर्पं कामं क्रोधं परिग्रहम् ।
विमुच्य निर्ममः शान्तो ब्रह्मभूयाय कल्पते ॥ 53

Endowed with a pure intellect, resolutely controlling his self,
relinquishing sense objects such as sound while rejecting
attraction and aversion, dwelling in solitude, eating little, with
speech, body, and mind under control, always intent upon the
discipline of meditation, ruled by dispassion, renouncing ego-
consciousness, force, arrogance, desire, anger, and possessions,
unselfish, and tranquil, he is made fit to become Brahman.

ब्रह्मभूतः प्रसन्नात्मा न शोचति न काङ्क्षति ।
समः सर्वेषु भूतेषु मद्भक्तिं लभते पराम् ॥ 54

Having become Brahman, with a serene self, he neither
grieves nor desires. Impartial to all beings, he attains supreme
devotion to me.

भक्त्या मामभिजानाति यावान्यश्चास्मि तत्त्वतः ।
ततो मां तत्त्वतो ज्ञात्वा विशते तदनन्तरम् ॥ 55

Through his devotion to me, he realizes my greatness and who I truly am. When he has truly come to know me, he enters me at once.

सर्वकर्माण्यपि सदा कुर्वाणो मद्व्यपाश्रयः ।
मत्प्रसादादवाप्नोति शाश्वतं पदमव्ययम् ॥ 56

And because he always performs all actions while taking refuge in me, he attains the eternal, imperishable state due to my grace.

चेतसा सर्वकर्माणि मयि संन्यस्य मत्परः ।
बुद्धियोगमुपाश्रित्य मच्चित्तः सततं भव ॥ 57

Mentally abandon all actions to me, be intent upon me, apply discipline to your intellect, and always keep your thoughts on me.

मच्चित्तः सर्वदुर्गाणि मत्प्रसादात्तरिष्यसि ।
अथ चेत्त्वमहंकारान्न श्रोष्यसि विनङ्क्ष्यसि ॥ 58

If you keep your thoughts on me, you will overcome all diffi-culties by my grace. But if, because of your ego-consciousness, you do not listen, you will perish.

यदहंकारमाश्रित्य न योत्स्य इति मन्यसे ।
मिथ्यैष व्यवसायस्ते प्रकृतिस्त्वां नियोक्ष्यति ॥ 59

If ego-consciousness leads you to think, "I will not fight," your resolve is futile. Nature will command you to fight.

स्वभावजेन कौन्तेय निबद्धः स्वेन कर्मणा ।
कर्तुं नेच्छसि यन्मोहात्करिष्यस्यवशोऽपि तत् ॥ 60

Son of Kunti, you are bound by your own karma, born of your nature! What your delusion tells you not to do, that you will do, even against your will.

ईश्वरः सर्वभूतानां हृद्देशेऽर्जुन तिष्ठति ।
भ्रामयन्सर्वभूतानि यन्त्रारूढानि मायया ॥ 61

The lord of all beings, Arjuna, abides in the heart, making all beings mounted on his waterwheel revolve with his wizardry.

तमेव शरणं गच्छ सर्वभावेन भारत ।
तत्प्रसादात्परां शान्तिं स्थानं प्राप्स्यसि शाश्वतम् ॥ 62

Go to him for refuge with all your being, Bharata! With his grace you will reach supreme peace, the eternal abode.

इति ते ज्ञानमाख्यातं गुह्यादगुह्यतरं मया ।
विमृश्यैतदशेषेण यथेच्छसि तथा कुरु ॥ 63

Thus I have imparted to you the most secret knowledge of all. When you have reflected upon this in its entirety, you can do what you like.

सर्वगुह्यतमं भूयः शृणु मे परमं वचः ।
इष्टोऽसि मे दृढमिति ततो वक्ष्यामि ते हितम् ॥ 64

Listen once more to my sublime word, the most secret of all. I love you deeply. Therefore I will tell you what is good for you.

मन्मना भव मद्भक्तो मद्याजी मां नमस्कुरु ।
मामेवैष्यसि सत्यं ते प्रतिजाने प्रियोऽसि मे ॥ 65

Turn your mind to me, be devoted to me, sacrifice to me, do homage to me, and you shall indeed come to me. I promise you truly, for you are dear to me.

सर्वधर्मान्परित्यज्य मामेकं शरणं व्रज ।
अहं त्वा सर्वपापेभ्यो मोक्षयिष्यामि मा शुचः ॥ 66

Abandon all laws and seek refuge in me alone! I will release you from all your evil actions, do not worry.

इदं ते नातपस्काय नाभक्ताय कदाचन ।
न चाशुश्रूषवे वाच्यं न च मां योऽभ्यसूयति ॥ 67

You must never mention this to a man who is not an ascetic, or has no devotion, or is disobedient, or bears a grudge against me.

य इदं परमं गुह्यं मद्भक्तेष्वभिधास्यति ।
भक्तिं मयि परां कृत्वा मामेवैष्यत्यसंशयः ॥ 68

He who explains this sublime secret to my devotees shall undoubtedly come to me, because he has shown the highest devotion to me.

न च तस्मान्मनुष्येषु कश्चिन्मे प्रियकृत्तमः ।
भविता न च मे तस्मादन्यः प्रियतरो भुवि ॥ 69

And no one among men is a better friend to me than he, nor will anyone else on earth be dearer to me than he.

अध्येष्यते च य इमं धर्म्यं संवादमावयोः ।
ज्ञानयज्ञेन तेनाहमिष्टः स्यामिति मे मतिः ॥ 70

I believe that I will be loved by him who recites this, our dialogue which is faithful to the law, as a sacrifice of knowledge.

श्रद्धावाननसूयश्च शृणुयादपि यो नरः ।
सोऽपि मुक्तः शुभाँल्लोकान्प्राप्नुयात्पुण्यकर्मणाम् ॥ 71

And the benevolent man of faith who listens to it, he too, should be released, reaching the blessed worlds of those whose actions are meritorious.

कच्चिदेतच्छ्रुतं पार्थ त्वयैकाग्रेण चेतसा ।
कच्चिदज्ञानसंमोहः प्रनष्टस्ते धनंजय ॥ 72

Son of Pritha, have you listened to this with complete concentration? Has the confusion caused by your ignorance been dispelled, Dhananjaya?'

अर्जुन उवाच ।
नष्टो मोहः स्मृतिर्लब्धा त्वत्प्रसादान्मयाच्युत ।
स्थितोऽस्मि गतसंदेहः करिष्ये वचनं तव ॥ 73

Arjuna said, 'My delusion is dispelled. By your grace, I remember who I am, Achyuta. I stand here free from doubt. I shall act on your words.'"

संजय उवाच ।
इत्यहं वासुदेवस्य पार्थस्य च महात्मनः ।
संवादमिममश्रौषमद्भुतं रोमहर्षणम् ॥ 74

Sanjaya said, "Thus I heard the wonderful and awe-inspiring dialogue between Vasudeva and the great-souled son of Pritha.

व्यासप्रसादाच्छ्रुतवानेतद्गुह्यमहं परम् ।
योगं योगेश्वरात्कृष्णात्साक्षात्कथयतः स्वयम् ॥ 75

By the grace of Vyasa, I heard about this supreme secret, Yoga, from the Lord of Yoga, from Krishna himself, who told it in person.

राजन्संस्मृत्य संस्मृत्य संवादमिममद्भुतम् ।
केशवार्जुनयोः पुण्यं हृष्यामि च मुहुर्मुहुः ॥ 76

O King, whenever I remember this wonderful and auspicious dialogue between Keshava and Arjuna, I rejoice over and over again.

तच्च संस्मृत्य संस्मृत्य रूपमत्यद्भुतं हरेः ।
विस्मयो मे महान्राजन्हृष्यामि च पुनः पुनः ॥ 77

And whenever I remember the miraculous form of Hari, I am filled with the greatest amazement, O King, and I rejoice again and again.

यत्र योगेश्वरः कृष्णो यत्र पार्थो धनुर्धरः ।
तत्र श्रीर्विजयो भूतिर्ध्रुवा नीतिर्मतिर्मम ॥ 78

Wherever there is Krishna, the Lord of Yoga; wherever there is the Son of Pritha, bow in hand; there surely will be fortune, victory, prosperity, and wise government. So I believe."

इति श्रीमहाभारते शतसाहस्रायां संहितायां श्रीमद्भगवद्गीतायां ब्रह्मविद्या-
शास्त्रे श्रीकृष्णार्जुनसंवादे मोक्षसंन्यासयोगारव्योऽष्टादशोऽध्यायः ॥

Thus ends the eighteenth chapter, entitled "The Reflection upon Liberation and Renunciation," in the instruction which teaches the sacred knowledge given by the exalted Krishna in his conversation with Arjuna, the auspicious Bhagavad Gita, which is in the work of a hundred thousand verses, the glorious *Mahabharata*.

Names and Nicknames

Achyuta Krishna. Means "unfallen, firm." Used as a name for Krishna in the Gita, but also used for others in the *Mahabharata*.

Aditya The sun.

Adityas A class of gods who are the sons of Aditi and Kashyapa. There are twelve of them, of whom Vishnu is the most important.

Agni The god of fire.

Airavata Indra's elephant.

Ananta One of the three kings of the serpents; the other two are Vasuki and Takshaka. Means "the infinite." Also known as Shesha.

Anantavijaya Yudhishthira's conch shell.

Arjuna The great archer and renowned hero of the *Mahabharata*. He is one of the five Pandu brothers (the Pandavas) who fight their evil Kuru cousins (the Kauravas) for the kingdom of Hastinapura. Arjuna is reputedly a son of Pandu by Kunti. However, Pandu lived apart from Kunti because of a curse, and Kunti had Arjuna by the god Indra.

Aryaman One of the Adityas.

Ashvattha The holy fig tree; also called the bo or pipal tree.

Ashvatthaman The son of Drona and Kripi. An elephant of the same name was killed during the battle to make Drona believe that his son had been killed.

Ashvins Ancient India's divine twins. They are the surgeons to the gods. Because of their beauty, they are often used in comparisons.

Asita Devala A seer. Also known as just Asita or Devala.

Best of the Bharatas Arjuna.

Best of the Kurus Arjuna. Although primarily a Pandava, he is also a Kaurava.

Bharata In the Gita, Arjuna and Dhritarashtra. In the plural, the descendants of Bharata.

Bhima One of the five Pandu brothers, also called Bhimasena. He is the son of Kunti and the reputed son of Pandu, but really the son of Vayu.

Bhishma The son of Shantanu and the river Ganges. He is a master of statecraft, and a great warrior fighting for the Kauravas.

Bhrigu A seer.

Brahma The creator god, the demiurge who fashions the world. *See also* Vishnu.

Brahma Sutras A work dealing with the knowledge of Brahman. One of the three central texts of Vedanta philosophy, the other two being the Upanishads and the Gita itself.

Brahman The primordial principle or shapeless substance of which the universe is made, and to which it returns.

Brahmic Brahman-related, sacred, or holy.

Brihaspati The priest (purohita) of the gods, and also the planet Jupiter.

Bull Among Men In the Gita, Arjuna and Shaibya.

Bull of the Bharatas Arjuna.

Chekitana A warrior of the Vrishni tribe.

Chitraratha The king of the Gandharvas.

Cow of Plenty A cow that belongs to the sage Vasishtha. She was produced by the churning of the Milk Ocean and is supposed to grant all wishes. Also the mother of all cows and a symbol of fertility.

Devadatta Arjuna's conch shell.

Dhananjaya Arjuna. Means "winner of wealth."

Dhrishtadyumna A warrior, and the son of Drupada. Killed by Ashvatthaman.

Dhrishtaketu The king of Chedi.

Dhritarashtra The brother of Pandu and Vidura. Born blind, he is the husband of Gandhari and the father of one hundred sons, the Kauravas. His eldest son is Duryodhana, whom the Pandavas fight against.

Draupadi The wife of the Pandavas.

Drona The military preceptor of both the Pandavas and the Kauravas, and the general of the Kauravas.

Drupada The king of Panchala and the father of Draupadi.

Duryodhana The eldest son of Dhritarashtra and the leader of the Kauravas.

Enemy Slayer Krishna.

Gandharvas Celestial musicians and singers in Indra's heaven.

Gandiva Arjuna's bow.

Ganges The holiest river of India.

Garuda A mythical bird and the mount of Vishnu.

Gayatri A poetic meter. It is also a specific verse in the Rigveda which every orthodox Brahmin must repeat at his morning and evening devotions.

Govinda Krishna. Means "protector of cows."

Gudakesha Arjuna. Means "thick-haired."

Hari Vishnu.

Hero of the Kurus Arjuna. Although primarily a Pandava, he is also a Kaurava.

Himalayas The world's highest mountains, located between India and Tibet. Means "place of snow."

Hrishikesha Krishna. Means "bristling-haired."

Ikshvaku A son of Manu Vaivasvata, he was the first king of the solar dynasty of Ayodhya.

Indra The king of the gods.

Jahnu An ancient king and sage. When the Ganges was brought down from heaven, it was forced to flow over the earth to the ocean and thence descend to the netherworld. In its course, it inundated the sacrificial ground of Jahnu, who drank up its waters but consented to discharge them from his ears. Hence the river Ganges is regarded as his daughter and called Jahnavi.

Janaka A king of Videha or Mithila.

Janardana Krishna.

Jayadratha A king fighting on the Kauravas' side.

Joy of the Kurus Arjuna. Although primarily a Pandava, he is also a Kaurava.

Kandarpa The god of love, also known as Kama or Kamadeva.

Kapila An ancient sage (identified by some with Vishnu and considered the founder of Sankhya).

Karna The king of Anga and the elder brother on his mother's side of the Pandu princes. He was the son of the sun god Surya by Kunti before her marriage to Pandu. Afraid of the censure of her relatives, Kunti abandoned the child in a river, where he was found by a charioteer named Adhiratha and nurtured by his wife Radha. Hence, Karna is sometimes called Sutaputra or Sutaja (son of a charioteer).

Kashi The holiest city in India, it sits on the banks of the Ganges in modern Uttar Pradesh. Also called Banaras or Varanasi.

Kauravas Descendants of Kuru. The term primarily refers to the sons of Dhritarashtra, who are the enemies of the Pandavas. However, the Pandavas are also, strictly speaking, Kauravas, since they all descend from Kuru.

Keshava Krishna.

Keshin A demon.

Kripa A son of Sharadvat, reared by Shantanu.

Krishna Arjuna's charioteer and an incarnation (avatar) of Vishnu.

Kunti The first of Pandu's two wives. Kunti was the daughter of a Yadava prince who let the childless Kuntibhoja adopt her. After receiving a charm from a sage, which enabled her to have children by any god she chose, her sons Yudhishthira, Bhima, and Arjuna were fathered by the gods Dharma, Vayu, and Indra respectively.

Kuntibhoja A Yadava prince who adopted Kunti.

Kuru The ancestor of the Kurus, a tribe. Also the name of their country, and the field on which the great battle is fought. Both the Kauravas proper and the Pandavas descend from Kuru. Technically, they are all Kauravas, but the term is only used for the hundred sons of Dhritarashtra, whereas the others are referred to as Pandavas.

Lord of the Earth Dhritarashtra. This is a general term for a king, but it is used twice for Dhritarashtra in the Gita.

Lord of Yoga Krishna.

Lotus Eyed Krishna.

Madhava Krishna.

Madhusudana Krishna. Means "destroyer of [the demon] Madhu."

Manipushpaka The conch shell of Sahadeva, one of the five Pandavas.

Manu In the Vedas, man par excellence, the representative man, and the father of the human race. In later mythology, the name Manu is especially applied to fourteen successive mythical progenitors and sovereigns of the earth, the seventh of which is Manu Vaivasvata, mentioned in verse 4.1. In verse 32.6, the four Manus are related to the four yugas, or ages of the world.

Margashirsha In the Hindu calendar, the month in which the full moon enters the constellation Mrigashiras. It corresponds to November-December in the Western calendar.

Marici A seer.

Maruts The storm gods, who are companions of Indra.

Meru A fabulous mountain, said to form the central point of the earth. It is surrounded by seven continents interspersed with oceans. Brahma resides on its summit.

Mighty-armed Prince In the Gita, Krishna or Arjuna. A generic epithet for warriors.

Nakula The twin brother of Sahadeva and half-brother of Arjuna, Bhima, and Yudhishthira. He is the fourth of the Pandu princes and the son of Madri, Pandu's second wife, and reputedly Pandu, but actually was the son of the Ashvins.

Narada A seer. In later mythology, he is a friend of Krishna and regarded as the inventor of the vina, or lute. In epic poetry, he is a Gandharva.

Pancajanya Krishna's conch shell.

Pandavas The sons of Pandu. They are Yudhishthira, Arjuna, Bhima, Nakula, and Sahadeva.

Pandu A son of Vyasa and one of the widows of Vichitravirya, he is the brother of Dhritarashtra and Vidura. He is ostensibly the father of the five Pandavas, although in reality they are the sons of various gods.

Paundra Bhima's conch shell.

Prahlada The king of the titans, who are not unlike the titans of Greek mythology.

Prajapati The creator. Means "lord of creatures." In later times, the name was also applied to Vishnu, Shiva, Time personified, the sun, fire, etc., as well as to lesser mythological figures.

Pritha Kunti.

Purujit The brother of Kuntibhoja. Fights on the side of the Pandavas.

Rama This name is shared by many figures in Hindu mythology. The most famous are Parashurama (Rama with the axe, the sixth incarnation of Vishnu), Ramachandra (the seventh incarnation of Vishnu, who killed the demon Ravana), and Balarama (the strong Rama, regarded as the eighth incarnation of Vishnu).

Rigveda The first Veda, consisting mostly of hymns in praise to the gods.

Rudra Shiva. Means "roarer, howler." In the Vedas, he is the god of tempests and the father and ruler of the Rudras and Maruts. It became a name for Shiva in classical Hinduism.

Rudras Storm gods who are sometimes identified with, or distinguished from, the Maruts.

Sadhyas A class of celestial beings.

Sahadeva The youngest of the five Pandu princes. He is the son of Madri and the reputed son of Pandu, but really the son of the Ashvins. The twin brother of Nakula.

Samaveda The third Veda, consisting of hymns for chanting during rituals. Most of the verses are taken from the Rigveda.

Sanjaya A bard. He is the narrator of the Bhagavad Gita.

Sankhya In the Gita, it means theory. Also one of the six darshanas (perspectives), or schools of Indic philosophy.

Satyaki Yuyudhana.

Saubhadra Matronymic of Abhimanyu, the son of Arjuna by Subhadra.

Scorcher of Enemies A general epithet, used in the Gita for Arjuna and Dhritarashtra.

Shaibya The king of the Shibis.

Shankara Shiva. *See also* Vishnu.

Shikhandi A son of Drupada, he was born as a female, but was changed into a male by a Yaksha. In the great war between the Pandavas and the Kauravas, he was instrumental in the killing of Bhishma, but afterwards was himself killed by Ashvatthaman.

Skanda Karttikeya, a god of war.

Slayer of Keshin Krishna.

Soma The intoxicating drink used in Vedic rituals. Also a name for the moon.

Somadatta A king.

Son of Dhritarashtra Duryodhana. In the plural, refers to the Kauravas.

Son of Kunti Arjuna.

Son of Pandu Epithet for any of the five sons of Pandu, but in the Gita, it refers to Arjuna. He is also called the ape-bannered son of Pandu.

Son of Pritha Arjuna in the Gita. In general, it is a patronymic for Yudhishthira, Bhima, and Arjuna.

Son of Vrishni Krishna, so called because he belonged to the Vrishni tribe (also known as the Yadavas).

Sughosha The conch shell of Nakula, one of the five Pandavas.

Supreme, the Brahman. Also referred to as the Supreme Reality.

Ucchaishravas Indra's horse. Produced by the churning of the Milk Ocean, and regarded as the archetype and king of horses.

Ushanas An ancient sage, in later times identified with Shukra, the teacher of the Asuras (demons).

Uttamaujas One of the warriors in the *Mahabharata*.

Varuna An Aditya. Varuna is one of the oldest of the Vedic gods. He is often regarded as the supreme deity, being styled "king of the gods" or "king of both gods and men" or "king of the universe."

Vasava Indra as chief of the Vasus.

Vasudeva Krishna.

Vasuki One of the three kings of the serpents. *See also* Ananta.

Vasus A particular class of gods whose chief was Indra, then later Agni and Vishnu.

Vayu The god of wind.

Vedanta One of the six darshanas (perspectives), or schools of Indic philosophy.

Vedas The collection of sacred hymns and ritual texts that are the earliest scriptures of Hinduism.

Vikarna A son of Dhritarashtra.

Vinata One of Kashyapa's wives, and the mother of Suparna, Aruna, and Garuda.

Virata An ancient king. The Pandavas, forced to conceal themselves during the thirteenth year of their exile, journeyed to his court and entered his service in various disguises.

Vishnu One of the principal deities of classical Hinduism, he is regarded as "the preserver." Along with Brahma "the creator" and Shiva "the destroyer", they constitute the trimurti, or triad. Although Vishnu comes second in the triad, he is identified with the supreme deity by his worshipers, and was later accorded the foremost place among the Adityas. He allows a portion of his essence to become incarnate on ten principal occasions in order to deliver the world from various great dangers.

Vishvedevas A class of gods. Means "the all-gods."

Vivasvat The sun. In epic poetry, regarded as the father of Manu Vaivasvata.

Vrishnis Krishna's tribe (also known as the Yadavas).

Vyasa A celebrated mythological sage and author. Often called Vedavyasa and regarded as the original compiler and arranger of the Vedas, he is also called Vadarayana, Badarayana, and Dvaipayana. When grown, he retired to the wilderness to lead the life of a hermit, but at his mother's request returned to become the husband of Vichitravirya's two childless widows, with whom he was the father of Dhritarashtra and Pandu. He was also the supposed compiler of the *Mahabharata* (yet also appears as a character within the epic), the *Puranas*, and other portions of Hindu sacred literature. But the name Vyasa, meaning "arranger, compiler," seems to have been given to any great editor or author.

Wolf Belly Bhima.

Yadava Krishna, so called because he belonged to the Yadava tribe (also known as the Vrishnis). Also simply a descendant of Yadu.

Yadu An ancient hero. Also the name of a country west of the Yamuna river.

Yakshas A class of supernatural beings, or spirits. Usually regarded as benevolent, but sometimes as malignant.

Yama The god of death.

Yoga In the Gita, most often means "mental discipline." Also one of the six darshanas (perspectives), or schools of Indic philosophy.

Yogi In the Gita, most often means "a master of mental discipline."

Yudhamanyu A warrior on the side of the Pandavas.

Yudhishthira The eldest of the five reputed sons of Pandu, but really the child of Kunti by the god Dharma, so he is often called Dharmaputra or Dharmaraja. He ultimately succeeded Pandu as king, first reigning over Indraprastha, and afterwards, when the Kuru princes were defeated, over Hastinapura.

Yuyudhana A son of Satyaka, he is a warrior who fights for the Pandavas.

Contributors

LARS MARTIN FOSSE holds a master's and doctorate from the University of Oslo, and also studied at the Universities of Heidelberg, Bonn, and Cologne. He has lectured at Oslo University on Sanskrit, Pali, Hinduism, text analysis, and statistics, and was a visiting fellow at Oxford University. He is one of Europe's most experienced translators.

YOGAVIDYA.COM is dedicated to publishing excellent and affordable books about Yoga. It is completely independent of any commercial, governmental, educational, or religious institutions.

Index

Page ranges in **bold** indicate a chapter by that title.

Vrishni, Son of (Krishna), 9, 36, 182
Vrishnis, 101, 183
Vyasa (Vedavyasa/Vadarayana/
    Badarayana/Dvaipayana), xvi,
    xviii, 96, 101, 174, 183

W
war, god of (Skanda), 98, 181
warriors, 18, 167. *See also* battle
water, 70, 98
wealth, 45, 47, 72, 145–147
wheel of life. *See* death-rebirth cycle
    (wheel of life)
wicked, the, 31, 41, 91
wickedness, 47. *See also* evil
Wilkins, Charles, xi, xx
wind, 70
wisdom
    attaining, purpose of, 140
    foundation of, 23–24, 25
    men of, 23, 34, 72–73, 158
    mental discipline for obtaining,
        26, 43
    origin of all, 100
Wolf Belly (Bhima), xiii, 2, 3, 4, 177,
    183
women
    attaining unity, 91
    corruption of, 9
work, doing one's, 168
world, origin of the, 70–71, 85–87
worship. *See also* devotion
    discipline of, 68, 75, 95, 117–118
    happiness from, 94–95
    peace attained through, 91
    undeviating, 87, 89–91, 94
    unity attained through, 90–91, 127

Y
Yadava (Krishna), 112, 183
Yadu, 183
Yakshas, 108, 183
Yama (god of death), 99, 112, 183
Yoga. *See also* meditation

achieving, 58–59, 65, 117
consequence of failure in, 66–67
defined, 183
discipline of, 48, 62–63, 65, 117
dominated by clarity, 165
equanimity as definition of, 22, 65
eternal and imperishable, 39–40
practice of, 60–63, 65
as sacrifice, 45
textual translation, xxiii
YogaVidya.com, xvii, xxi
yogi(s)
    characteristics of, 55, 58, 60, 120
    death-rebirth cycle, 82–83
    defined, xxiii
    discipline in, 60–62, 68
    perfect, 64, 67–68
    renunciation of attachment, 52
    sacrifices offered by, 45
    stainless, 63–64
Yudhamanyu, 2, 183
Yudhishthira (Dharmaputra/
    Dharmaraja), xiii–xiv, 183
Yuyudhana (Satyaki), 2, 183